COUNT

Thirty Rides in

Anna Pond
&
Simon Shaw

TWO WHEELS

G000256858

COUNTY RIDES

Thirty Rides in Thirteen Counties

Anne Pond

&

Simon Shaw

Simon Shaw and Anna Pond are the couple behind Bike 1. They met on bicycles in 1987 and have since covered many miles together - on numerous cycling holidays as well as on their own organised rides.

Bike 1 was born during a walk in Windsor Great Park with Martin Neville, a good friend of Simon and Anna. Their first organised ride took place in January 1992, when 54 riders assembled at the Station Cafe in Alton, Hampshire.

The idea is to discover a different County every month, with a choice of mileages, full back-up facilities, plenty of tea and cakes and the enjoyable atmosphere generated by kindred spirits. The routes selected for **COUNTY RIDES - Thirty rides in Thirteen Counties** represent some of the best cycling to be had in England. It is a real pleasure to make these routes available for all cyclists to discover and enjoy the beauty of the English countryside - at your own pace and in your own time.

For information on their latest programme of rides please write to:
Bike 1, PO Box 105, Fleet, Hampshire, GU13 8YR.

First published in 1994 by

Two Wheels - an imprint of
Two Heads Publishing
12A Franklyn Suite
The Priory
Haywards Heath
West Sussex
RH16 3LB

Copyright © **Two Wheels** 1994

All rights reserved. No part of this publication may be
reproduced or transmitted in any form or by any means,
electronic or mechanical including photocopying,
recording or any information storage or retrieval system,
without prior permission in writing from the publishers.

A catalogue record for this book is available from the
British Library.

Every effort has been made to ensure the accuracy of
information in this book. Details such as Rights of Way,
tracks, roads, places to see and refreshment stops may
be subject to change and the authors and publishers
cannot accept liability for any errors or omissions.

ISBN   1-898933-00-6

Cover Design by David Spencer.
Maps by Julie Sinclair.
Illustrations by Doreen Pond.
Printed & bound by Caldra House Ltd., Hove, Sussex

CONTENTS

INTRODUCTION

The County Rides

The routes in this book are designed to allow the cyclist to discover and explore the beauty of the English countryside. They can be cycled in their entirety or used as a basic route to which you can add your own detours, start and finish points. Use them for cycle touring, a day out in the countryside, for fitness and exercise, for a weekend away, as a solo rider or in a group.

The routes concentrate on relatively traffic-free areas - the country lanes and tracks which make up England's dense map of unclassified roads. Abandoned by motorists for being too narrow, too slow or simply because they are unsignposted, these lanes have become a haven for cycling.

Thirteen counties are covered in this book. All the routes are easy to reach by car or by train. They offer a choice of distances so you can decide how far you want to cycle either before you set off, when you start or at the points on the ride where the routes divide.

Each set of ride directions is preceded by a general description of the ride and the area it covers, map details, the distances to choose from, the start point, railway access, places to see and refreshment stops.

Timings

No timings are given for the various routes in the book. An average road speed, hills notwithstanding, can vary between 6 and 12 miles per hour therefore the length of time taken will vary with the fitness and aims of the rider, the weather conditions, the terrain and how often and for how long you stop. The best approach is not to overestimate your fitness and ability - take it easy and enjoy the rides by cycling at your own pace.

Maps

A sketch map accompanies each ride. Many of them cover more than one page but it is clear where they join. The maps provide an overview of the ride, and, in conjunction with the ride directions, will help you follow the route. We recommend that you equip yourself with the appropriate Ordnance Survey Landranger map for the area as this will assist with detailed route finding and working out detours and options.

The actual route to be followed is hatched on the map with arrows showing the direction of travel. Mileage points are shown as are the places to see and refreshment stops mentioned in the information pages after the overview of the ride.

Start & Finish Points

Every ride has to start somewhere so we have included a recommended start point. All the routes are easy to reach by car and by train, or by bike if you live nearby. Most of the start points have free parking. The suggested start point is just that - the ride directions are written in such a way to provide maximum flexibility - you could start and finish the ride wherever it is most convenient for you. Railway stations, either on or close to the route, are mentioned before each set of ride directions and provide ideal alternative access points.

Railway Access

All the routes are accessible by train, with a station either at or close to the recommended start point or elsewhere on the route. Unfortunately, the rules and regulations on taking a bike on a train are complex and often far from clear. For instance, Network South East alone consists of nine divisions, each of which has responsibility for its own cycle carriage policy. Intercity trains will carry bikes but numbers are restricted and reservations essential. Regional Railways make a modest charge. The best advice is to check with your local railway station before you set off.

Network South East provide a comprehensive and helpful information leaflet entitled 'Cycling by Train on Network South East.' Regional Railways do a 'Cycling by Train' leaflet, available from main stations or by telephoning 081 200 0200.

Places to See & Refreshment Stops

Brief details of a selection of places to see and where to stop for refreshments, on or close to the route, are included in the information pages for each county, before the ride directions. Bear in mind that this is only a selection and that every place mentioned is also marked on the map to help you plan your stops. The address and telephone number for the local Tourist Information Office is also included and we recommend that you give them a call if you plan a weekend ride or would like further information on what there is to see in a particular area.

Ride Directions

The ride directions are designed to be detailed, clear and functional. The first column is the mileage point from the start. The next column will contain the word RIGHT, LEFT or CONT - for straight on or continue - and describes the direction you cycle at the junction at this mileage point. Every direction is then followed by two sentences. The first sentence describes the junction you are at - so you know you are in the right place. The second is **in bold type** and is the instruction to the next junction where you go RIGHT, LEFT or CONT. This sentence will tell you precisely how far that turn is and how you will recognise the junction. For example:

1·6   LEFT signposted Cardington 4. **Cycle 1·5m to T junction end**.

At 1·6 miles from the start you turn LEFT at the junction signposted 'Cardington 4.' You then continue cycling for 1·5 miles, ignoring other junctions, to the T junction at the end of the road you are on. The next mileage point will therefore be 3·1 (1·6 + 1·5) and will tell you the direction to take and so on.

The easiest way to make smooth progress is to read the directions in twos and threes, depending upon the intricacy of the route.

Places to see and refreshment stops are mentioned when they are material to the ride directions. Mention is also made of points at which routes divide. As there is a choice of distances for most counties there is a separate set of ride directions for each distance, even though both a short and long ride may share the same portion of the route. Once you have chosen a distance you need only follow the ride directions for that distance.

Checklists

It is beyond the scope of this book to include a mass of detail on cycle maintenance and how to ride. There are plenty of books available on such topics should you feel the need for them. What we have included is quick and easy checklists to cover preparations before you set out on a ride, what to take and guidelines for when you are on the road.

CHECKLISTS

Before You Go

✗ familiarise yourself with the proposed route

✗ allow sufficient time and don't overestimate your ability and fitness

✗ identify refreshment stops and places to see

✗ tell someone where you are going and when you expect to return

✗ check your bike: brakes, tyres, chain, gears and riding position

What to Take

✗ waterproof and warm clothing, plus enough space to store them

✗ spare inner tubes and a puncture repair kit

✗ tyre levers and tools to remove wheels if they are not quick release

✗ a small tool kit, a pump, working lights and a bicycle lock

✗ a small first aid kit, lip-salve and water resistant sun block

✗ a map, a compass, money, food & drink

On the Road

✗ ride confidently and responsibly

✗ stay alert on country lanes - you may be crossing much busier roads

✗ know your Rights of Way, if in doubt find out

✗ bridleways are generally open to cyclists. If local bylaws prohibit cycling this should be signposted

✗ always give way to horses and walkers

✗ designated cycle paths should be waymarked with a sign showing a bicycle symbol

✗ cycling is not permitted on pavements, public footpaths and open land

✗ behave responsibly and courteously, do nothing to erode hard-won access rights

✗ consider wearing a helmet when cycling off-road

✗ when cycling in a group, do not bunch and respect other road users

✗ respect and protect wildlife, plants, trees and the environment

✗ use gates (fasten behind you) and stiles to cross fences, hedges and walls

✗ do not stray from rights of way across farmland

✗ take your litter home and guard against fire

✗ make no unnecessary noise

VILLAGES AROUND BEDFORD & THE OUSE VALLEY

This route starts and finishes at Haynes, south of Bedford. Both routes are generally fast and flat, through pleasant open countryside on roads that are often traffic-free. The shorter route covers a 19 mile loop south-east of Bedford on very quiet minor roads and passes through Old Warden. Massive airship hangers dominate the scene at Cardington, as does the Whitbread family, of brewing fame. Samuel Whitbread's initials appear on many of the houses, like seals of approval.

The 53 mile route surrounds Bedford and is again on minor roads and country lanes. It crosses the Great Ouse river then continues on the west side of the Ouse Valley. After 15 miles the long route passes through Stagsden, a pretty village of thatched and stone-built cottages, part of an established agricultural community with many farms surrounded by gentle hills and green fields. Church Lane leads to Stagsden Bird Gardens, pleasantly set in eight acres of woodland.

This is an easy to follow route and the miles seem to slip by effortlessly.

Map	OS LR 153 Bedford, Huntingdon & area.
Distance	19 or 53 miles.
Start/Finish	Village Hall, Northwood End Road, Haynes.

Railway Access

Bedford - trains from London St Pancras.

Biggleswade - 2.5m from the south-east corner of the route, trains from Kings Cross.

Places to see

Bedford Museum, Castle Lane, Bedford. A local history and natural history museum, free admission.

Cecil Higgins Gallery & Museum, Castle Close, Bedford. An award winning Victorian mansion, recreated to give lived-in authenticity.

Stagsden Bird Gardens, 150 species of birds in eight acres of woodland.

Jordans Mill, Biggleswade. Home of the famous cereal bars and muesli, located 2 miles off the route. Open to the public and has a tea-room and shop.

Shuttleworth Collection, Old Warden. Home of a superb collection of aircraft and vehicles.

Tourist Information Office, St Paul's Square, Bedford 0234 215226.

Refreshments

Five Bells PH, Cople - 7.5m short route.

The Mad Dog PH, Odell - 23m.

Bell Inn, Odell - 23.4m.

The Jackel PH, Thurleigh - 30.8m long route.

Golden Cross PH, Blunham - 38.8m long route.

Hare & Hounds PH, Old Warden - 13m short, 47.3m long.

The Kings Arms PH, Cardington - 6.4m short route.

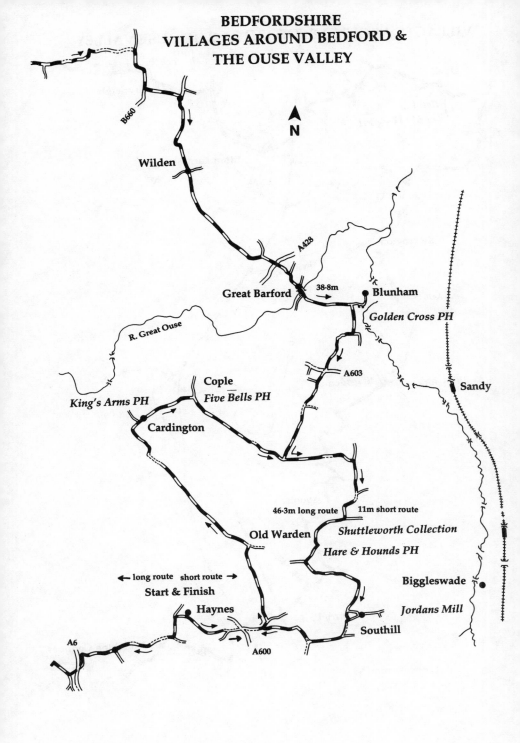

VILLAGES AROUND BEDFORD & THE OUSE VALLEY

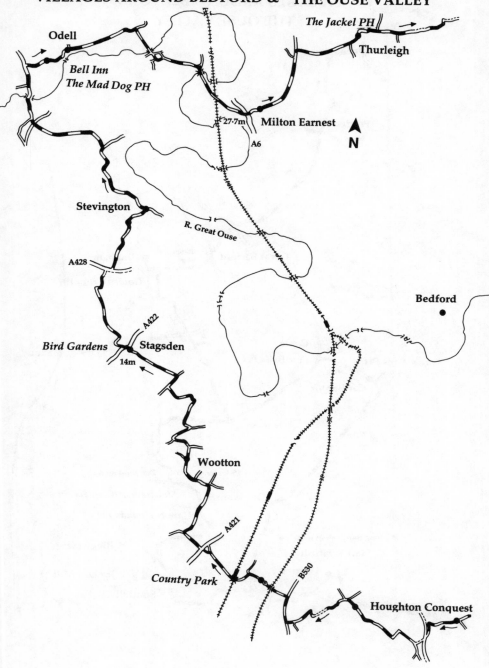

BEDFORDSHIRE - 19 MILE ROUTE

0.0   LEFT   out of hall. **Cycle 1·1 m to crossroads end.**
(The longer route turns right out of the hall).

1·1   CONT   over crossroads signposted Southill & Old Warden
2 ½. **Cycle 0·5m to left turn signposted
Cardington 4 ¾.**

1·6   LEFT   signposted Cardington 4 ¾. **Cycle 1·5m to
T junction end.**

3·1   LEFT   at T junction signposted Cardington 3 ½ & Bedford
6¼. **Cycle 4·4m to T junction end.**

6·4   The Kings Arms PH in Cardington village.

7·5   RIGHT   at T junction signposted Northill 3 & Biggleswade 7.
Cycle 3·3m to T junction end.
The Five Bells PH in Cople village.

10·8   RIGHT   at T junction signposted Ickwell 1 ½ into Ickwell
road. **Cycle 1·2m to T junction with grass triangle.**

The long route rejoins here.

10·9   The Crown PH.

12·0   RIGHT   at T junction, grass triangle signposted Old Warden
¾ & Southill 3. **Cycle 1·3m to left turn signposted
Southill 2 & Broom 3 ¼.**

13·0   The Hare & Hounds PH.

13·3   LEFT   signposted Southill 2 & Broom 3 ¾.
Cycle 1·6m to T junction end in Southill.

14·9   RIGHT   at T junction signposted Ireland 1 ¾ & Shefford 3 ½
into School Lane. **Cycle 0·2m to T junction & grass
triangle.**

15·1   RIGHT   at T junction & grass triangle signposted Ireland 1 ¾
& Shefford 3. **Cycle 0·5m to T junction end.**
The White Horse PH.

15·6 RIGHT at T junction signposted Ireland & Shefford 2 ½ .
**Cycle 0·6m to right turn signposted Ireland ½
& Old Warden 2.**

16·2 RIGHT signposted Ireland ½ & Old Warden.
Cycle 1m to T junction end.
The Black Horse Inn.

17·2 LEFT at T junction signposted Haynes 1 ¾.
Cycle 0·4m to crossroads end.

17·6 CONT over crossroads signposted Haynes.
Cycle 1·1m to right turn into Haynes village hall.

18·3 The Greyhound PH.

18·7 RIGHT into Haynes Village Hall.

End of 19 m route.

BEDFORDSHIRE - 53 MILE ROUTE

0·0   RIGHT out of hall. **Cycle 0·2m to T junction end.**

0·2   LEFT   at T junction signposted Haynes.
Cycle 0·4m to T junction end.

0·6   RIGHT at T junction signposted Haynes & Church End.
Cycle 2m to junction at A6.

2·6   LEFT   at T junction signposted London A6.
Cycle to 1st right for Haynes West End.

2·7   RIGHT signposted Haynes West End ½. **Cycle 0·2m to
right turn by grass triangle.**

2·9   RIGHT at grass triangle. **Cycle 1·6m to T junction end.**

4·5   LEFT   at T junction signposted Ampthill 3.
Cycle 1·4m to T junction end.

5·9   RIGHT at T junction signposted Bedford 6. **Cycle 0·4m to
1st left signposted Stewartby.**

6·3   LEFT   signposted Stewartby. **Cycle 0·5m to roundabout.**

6·8   CONT   over roundabout signposted Marston Moretaine.
Cycle 0·4m to roundabout.

7·2   LEFT   at roundabout signposted Marston Moretaine 2 ½ &
Station. **Cycle 1·1m to T junction**

8·3   LEFT   at T junction signposted Marston Moretaine ¼. **Cycle
0·1m to 1st right signposted Wootton Green 1.**

8·4   RIGHT signposted Wootton Green 1. **Cycle 0·5m to
T junction with grass triangle.**

8·9   RIGHT at T junction & grass triangle signposted Wootton 1,
Kempston 3 ¾ & Bedford 5¾. **Cycle 1m to 1st left
signposted Hall End & Wootton Church.**

9·9   LEFT   signposted Hall End & Wootton Church into Church
Road. **Cycle 0·9m to T junction with grass triangle.**

10·8 LEFT   at T junction signposted Wood End ¾ & Bourne End
1 ½. **Cycle 0·4m to T junction end.**

11·2 RIGHT at T junction signposted Wood End ¼ & Kempston 2. **Cycle 0·4m to T junction end.**

11·6 LEFT at T junction signposted Stagsden 3 into Tithe Road. **Cycle 1·2m to T junction & grass triangle.**

12·8 RIGHT at T junction & grass triangle signposted Bromham 2 into West End Road. **Cycle 0·3m to 1st left signposted Stagsden 2.**

13·1 LEFT signposted Stagsden 2. **Cycle 0·9m to T junction.**

14·0 LEFT at T junction signposted Stagsden 1 & Astwood 2 ½. **Cycle 0·6m to 1st right turn signposted Stagsden & Bird Gardens.**

14·6 RIGHT signposted Stagsden ½. **Cycle 0·5m to left turn signposted Stevington 3 & Turvey 4.**

15·1 LEFT signposted Stevington 3 & Turvey 4 into Church Lane, just past Royal George PH. **Cycle 1·8m to T junction end with A428.**

16·9 RIGHT at T junction signposted Stevington, Bromham & Bedford A428. **Cycle 0·2m to 1st left turn signposted Stevington 1 ½.**

17·1 LEFT signposted Stevington 1 ½. **Cycle 1·4m to T junction end in Stevington**

18·5 LEFT at T junction signposted Pavenham 2 ½ & Carlton 3. **Cycle 1·7m to left turn signposted Carlton 1 ¾ & Harrold 2 ½. Royal George & Red Lion PH.**

20·2 LEFT signposted Carlton 1 ¾ & Harrold 2 ½. **Cycle 2m through Carlton village to right turn in Harrold signposted Odell ¾ & Sharnbrook 3.**

22·7 RIGHT signposted Odell ¾ and Sharnbrook 3 into High Street. **Cycle 2·3m through Odell village to right turn signposted Felmersham ½ & Radwell 1 ½.**

23·4 The Bell Inn Odell village.

25·0 RIGHT signposted Felmersham ½ & Radwell 1 ½. **Cycle 2·7m to T junction with A6.**

26·4   The Swan PH.

27·7   RIGHT   at T junction signposted Clapham 2 & Bedford A6. **Cycle to 1st left turn signposted Thurleigh 3.** Tea room (from 2pm) & The Queens Head Hotel.

27·8   LEFT   signposted Thurleigh 3 into Thurleigh Road. **Cycle 1·6m to first right turn signposted Thurleigh 1 ½ & Bolnhurst 4.**

29·4   RIGHT   signposted Thurleigh 1 ½, Bolnhurst 4 into Milton Road. **Cycle 3·8m to T junction at B660**

30·8   The Jackel PH in Thurleigh village.

33·2   RIGHT   at T junction signposted Bolnhurst Top End, Ravensden 3 ½ & Bedford 6 ½ B660. **Cycle 0·8m to 1st left turn signposted Colmwort & Little Staughton.**

33·3   The Plough PH.

34·0   LEFT   signposted Colmworth 1 ¾ & Little Staughton into New Road. **Cycle 0·7m to T junction end.**

34·7   RIGHT   at T junction signposted Wilden 1 ½, Great Barford 3 & Blunham 5 by Wheatsheaf PH. **Cycle 1·5m to staggered crossroads end.**

36·2   CONT   at staggered crossroads (right then left) signposted Great Barford 2 & Blunham 4 into Barford Road. **Cycle 2·6m to crossroads end with A428.**

38·8   CONT   over crossroads with A428 signposted Blunham into High Street. **Cycle 0·7m to traffic lights end.** Shop & Golden Cross PH.

39·5   CONT   at traffic lights and over bridge. **Cycle 1m to a right turn signpostedMogerhanger 1 ½ in Blunham.** The Anchor Inn.

40·5   RIGHT   signpostedMogerhanger 1 ½ into Station Road. **Cycle 0·6m to a right turn signposted Mogerhanger 1 by a small grass triangle.**

41·1   RIGHT   at grass triangle signposted Mogerhanger 1 &

Bedford 7. **Cycle 0·9m to staggered crossroads end in Mogerhanger village.**

42·0 CONT at staggered crossroads signposted St Johns Home ½ & Northill 3 into St Johns Road. **Cycle 1·9m to T junction end.** The Guinea PH.

43·9 LEFT at T junction signposted Northill 1 ¼. **Cycle 1·2m to T junction end.**

45·1 RIGHT at T junction signposted Ickwell 1 ½ into Ickwell road. **Cycle 1·2m to T junction with grass triangle.** The Crown PH.

46·3 RIGHT at T junction & grass triangle signposted Old Warden ¾ & Southill 3. **Cycle 1·3m to left turn signposted Southill 2 & Broom 3 ¼ in Old Warden.**

47·3 The Hare & Hounds PH.

47·6 LEFT signposted Southill 2 & Broom 3 ¾ **Cycle 1·6m to T junction end in Southill.**

49·2 RIGHT at T junction signposted Ireland 1 ¾ & Shefford 3 ½ into School Lane. **Cycle 0·2m to T junction end with grass triangle.**

49·4 RIGHT at T junction with grass triangle signposted Ireland 1 ½ & Shefford 3. **Cycle 0·3m to T junction end.**

49·7 RIGHT at T junction signposted Ireland & Shefford 2 ½. **Cycle 0·6m to right turn signposted Ireland ½ & Old Warden 2.**

50·3 RIGHT signposted Ireland & Old Warden. **Cycle 1m to T junction.**

51·3 LEFT at T junction signposted Haynes 1 ¾. **Cycle 0·4m to crossroads.**

51·7 CONT over crossroads signposted Haynes. **Cycle 1·1m to right turn into Haynes Village Hall.**

52·8 RIGHT into hall.

End of 53m route.

THE ROYAL WINDSOR RIDE

This parkland ride starts and finishes in Sunningdale. It is easy to reach from the railway station, where car parking is available, and is simple to extend by means of a detour to Windsor and the Thames.

The park is truly wonderful for cycling as the ancient oaks and deer are more prevalent than the ubiquitous car - it is car-free, except for residents. The route enters Windsor Great Park through the Blacknest Gate and all the ride is on a tarmac surface. Cross the western edge of Virginia Water, under High Flyer's Hill, past the famous polo grounds and across Smith's Lawn. The unrestricted view down The Long Walk towards Winsdsor is a delight - the Castle dominates all around it. The most striking sight of all is the copper statue of George III astride his horse, from which you can overlook magnificent parkland and the western approaches to London with a twist of the head.

The route continues through The Village and down Dukes Lane to leave the park at Prince Consorts gate. You can then decide whether to return to Sunningdale or do another lap of the park.

Map	OS LR 175 Reading & Windsor. OS Pathfinder 1189 & 1173.
Distance	18 miles.
Start/Finish	Sunningdale Village Hall, Church Road.

Railway Access

Sunningdale - trains from London Waterloo.

Ascot - 2m west of the start, trains from Waterloo.

Places to see

Windsor - to the north of the route. See the town, the Castle and Eton.

Windsor Great Park - the ride goes through this magnificent parkland and Virginia Water, an excellent picnic stop is close by.

River Thames & Runnymede - If you leave the park at the Fox & Hounds pub the historic banks of the Thames at Runnymede is less than a mile away. It would then be worth cycling north alongside the river and back to the park through Old Windsor.

Tourist Information Office, Thames Street, Windsor 0753 852010.

Refreshments

The Chukka PH, just before Blacknest Gate - 1m.

Fox & Hounds PH, - Windsor Park - 3.8m.

General Stores, The Village - 5.5m.

Royal Oak PH, Station Road, Sunningdale - 18m.

Tylers Bar & Restaurant, off the A30, Sunningdale - start.

BERKSHIRE
THE ROYAL WINDSOR RIDE

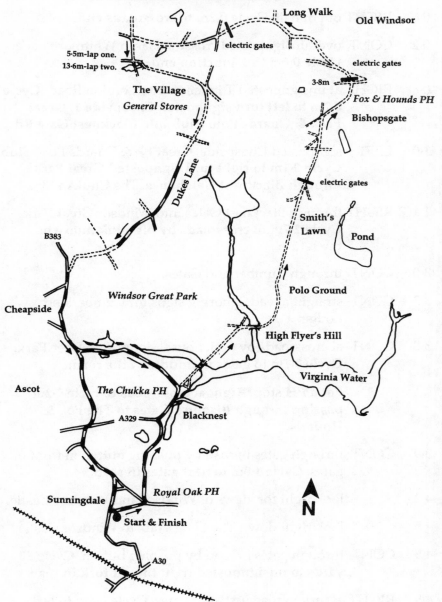

Long Walk

Old Windsor

electric gates

5·5m-lap one.
13·6m-lap two.

electric gates

3·8m

The Village
General Stores

Fox & Hounds PH

Bishopsgate

electric gates

Smith's
Lawn

Pond

B383

Windsor Great Park

Polo Ground

Cheapside

High Flyer's Hill

Virginia Water

Ascot

The Chukka PH

Blacknest

A329

Royal Oak PH

Sunningdale

Start & Finish

A30

N

BERKSHIRE - 18M ROUTE

0·0   RIGHT out of hall. **Cycle 0·2m to crossroads end.**

0·2   CONT over unsignposted crossroads into Whitmore Lane. **Cycle 0·6m to T junction end.**

0·8   RIGHT at unsignposted T junction into London Road. **Cycle 0·2m to left turn signposted Cheapside 1, Great Park & Guards Polo Club into Blacknest Gate Rd.**

1·0   LEFT signposted Cheapside, Great Pk & Guards Polo Club. **Cycle 0·1m to right turn signposted Great Park through Blacknest Gatehouse.** The Chukka PH.

1·1   RIGHT through Blacknest Gates into Windsor Great Park. **Cycle 2·7m to crossroads by big pink house on the left.**

3·0   CONT through Cumberland Gates.

3·3   CONT straight ahead, ignoring signs for Cumberland Lodge.

3·8   CONT at crossroads by pink house, signposted Deer Park. **Cycle 0·1m to gates in middle of the road.**

        For a PH stop. Right at crossroads & cycle 0·2m passing through Bishop's Gates to The Fox & Hounds.

3·9   CONT through gates in road by pushing button in front of gates. **Cycle 1·0m to next gates in road.**

4·2   look right for views of Windsor and Windsor Castle.

4·5   look right down The Long Walk to Windsor Castle.

4·9   CONT through gates in road by pushing button. **Cycle 50 yards to unsignposted right turn at fork in road.**

4·9   RIGHT at fork in road just after gates. **Cycle 0·6m to left turn signposted The Village Shop, The Village, York Club, Royal School & Cumberland Lodge.**

5·5 LEFT signposted The Village Shop, The Village, York Club, Royal School & Cumberland Lodge. **Cycle 0·2m to crossroads.**

5·7 LEFT at crossroads signposted The Village Shop, Cumberland Lodge & The Village. **Cycle 0·5m to crossroads.**

6·2 RIGHT at crossroads after 'Caution crossroads' sign. **Cycle 1·9m to left turn at unsignposted T junction with main road.**

8·1 LEFT after Prince Consorts Gates at T junction with main road. **Cycle 1·1m along the main road to left turn into Mill Lane.**

9·2 LEFT intoMill Lane. **Cycle 0·8m to left turn at Blacknest Gate into Windsor Great Park.**

10·0 LEFT through Blacknest Gate into Windsor Great Park. **Cycle 2·7m to crossroads by large pink house.**

11·9 CONT through Cumberland Gates.

12·7 CONT over crossroads by pink house on the left signposted Deer Park. **Cycle 0·1m to gates in middle of road.**

For a PH stop. Right at crossroads & cycle 0·2m passing through Bishop's Gates to The Fox and Hounds.

12·8 CONT through gates in road by pushing button in front of gates. **Cycle 1·0m to next gates in road.**

13·8 CONT through gates in road by pushing button. **Cycle 50 yards to unsignposted left turn at fork in road.**

13·8 LEFT at fork in road after gates. **Cycle 0·4m to unsignposted crossroads.**

14·2 CONT straight over unsignposted crossroads. **Cycle 1·9m to left turn at unsignposted T junction with main road.**

15·7 CONT through Prince Consort's Gates.

16·1 LEFT at unsignposted T junction with main road. **Cycle 1·1m to staggered crossroads end.**

17·2 CONT right then left at staggered crossroads signposted Sunningdale 1, Civil Service College & Sunningdale Park, into Silwood Road. **Cycle 0·7m to unsignposted left turn into Church Road.**

17·2 The Cannon PH.

17·8 The Royal Oak PH.

17·9 LEFT into Church Road. **Cycle short distance to right turn into hall.**

18·0 RIGHT into Sunningdale Village Hall.

End of 18m route.

UNSPOILT TERRITORY AROUND CHELMSFORD

A choice of three routes on quiet, traffic-free lanes through open countryside, which although being mainly flat, has much to offer. Many of the lanes are single track and the ride is dotted with attractive villages of traditional pink-washed cottages. All routes start south of Braintree at the County Show Ground although there are numerous good access points for alternative start points. It is easy to extend or shorten the routes at will.

The two shorter routes cover the area north of Chelmsford - the 16m through Pleshey and the 29m through the villages of High and Good Easter. The long route heads south through Danbury, west past Hanningfield Reservoir to Ingatestone, then north to the Easters to complete a glorious circumnavigation of the countryside surrounding Chelmsford.

Map	OS LR 167 Chelmsford, Harlow & area.
Distance	16, 29 or 58 miles.
Start/Finish	Essex County Showground, Great Leighs, Chelmsford.

Railway Access

Ingatestone - south on the route, from London Liverpool St.

Hatfield Paverel - east on the route, from London Liverpool St.

Chelmsford - centre of the route, from London Liverpool St.

Billericay - south on the route, on the Southend line from Liverpool St.

Places to see

Chelmsford & Essex Museum, Oakland Park, Moulsham Street, Chelmsford. Permanent exhibitions of local and social history.

Danbury Country Park, Danbury. Woodland, lakes and ornamental gardens.

Pleshey. See the great mound (60 feet high and 900 feet circumference) on which Geoffrey de Mandeville's castle once stood.

The Easters. The villages of Good and High Easter.

Tourist Information Office, County Hall, Market Road, Chelmsford 0245 283400.

Refreshments

Leather Bottle PH, Pleshey - 7.4m, 15m route.

Star PH, Good Easter - 12.4m, 29m route.

Punch Bowl PH, Cork & Bell Inn, High Easter - 17.1m, 29m route.

The Bell PH, Rettendon - 19.8m, 29m route.

Cafe, Star PH, Ingatestone - 29.3m, 58m route.

ESSEX UNSPOILT TERRITORY AROUND CHELMSFORD

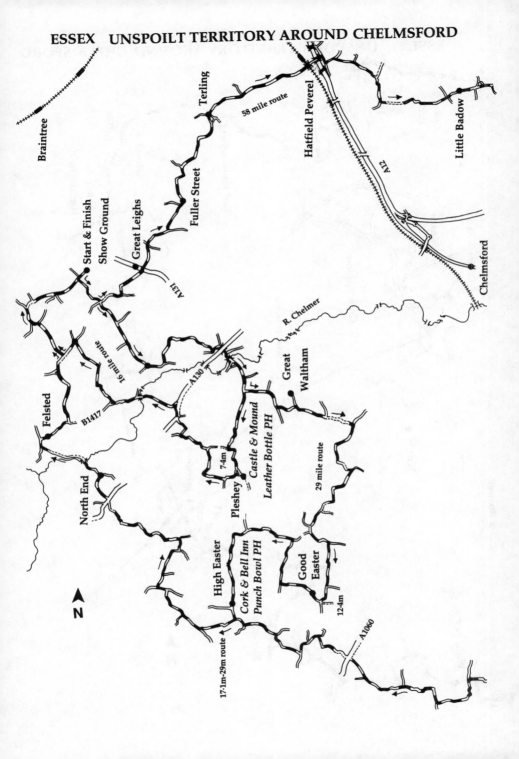

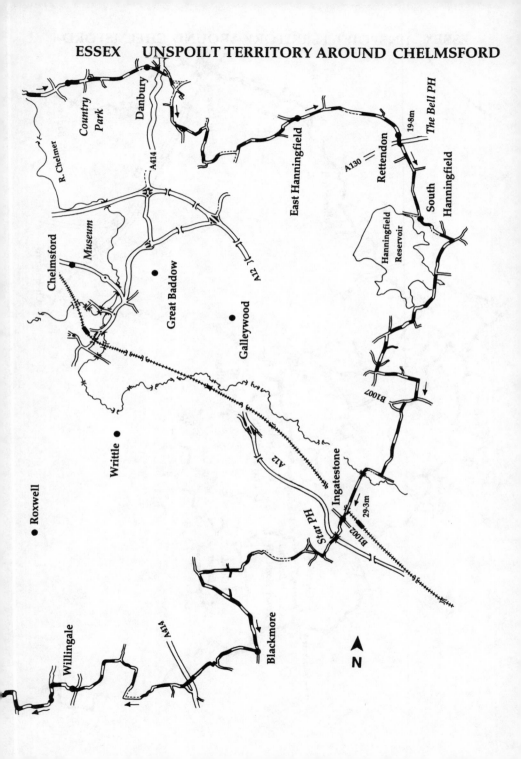

ESSEX   UNSPOILT TERRITORY AROUND CHELMSFORD

ESSEX - 16M ROUTE

0·0   RIGHT out of show ground entrance from the same entrance you came in at. **Cycle 0·3m to left turn signposted Littley Green.**

0·3   LEFT   into Hornells Corner signposted Littley Green. **Cycle 0·7m to staggered crossroads end.**

The 59m route turns left here, you continue.

1·0   CONT over staggered crossroads signposted Littley Green into Howe Street. **Cycle 2m to left turn by grass triangle signposted, Old Shaws.**

2·6   Compasses Inn.

3·0   LEFT   at grass triangle signposted Old Shaws. **Cycle 0·2m to small unsignposted T junction.**

3·2   RIGHT at small unsignposted T junction. **Cycle 0·3m to small unsignposted T junction.**

3·5   RIGHT at small unsignposted T junction. **Cycle 1·1m to T junction end.**

4·6   LEFT   at T junction signposted Howe Street & Little Walthams. **Cycle 0·2m to T junction end.**

4·8   RIGHT at T junction signposted Howe Street & The Walthams. **Cycle 0·1m to T junction end.**

4·9   RIGHT at T junction signposted Howe Street & Pleshey. **Cycle 0·3m to T junction end.**

5·2   LEFT   at unsignposted T junction. **Cycle 0·3m to right turn signposted Pleshey 2.**

5·5   RIGHT signposted Pleshey 2. **Cycle 2m to unsignposted right turn in Pleshey.**

5·8   *The 29m route turns left here, you continue.*

7·4   The Leather Bottle PH.

7·5   RIGHT immediately after Pleshey Post Office. **Cycle 0·1m to left turn signposted Pleshey Grange.**

7·6 LEFT signposted Pleshey Grange. **Cycle 0·3m to right turn signposted Ford End.**

7·9 RIGHT signposted Ford End. **Cycle 0·9m to T junction end.**

8·8 LEFT at T junction signposted Ford End & Felsted. **Cycle 0·6m to unsignposted right turn.**

9·4 RIGHT unsignposted. **Cycle 0·5m to T junction with A130.**

9·9 RIGHT at unsignposted T junction with A130. **Cycle 0·1m to left turn signposted Felsted B1417.**

10·0 LEFT signposted Felsted B1417. **Cycle 0·1m to T junction end.**

10·1 LEFT at T junction signposted Felsted 2. **Cycle 1·2m to right turn signposted Leez Priory & Rayne.**

11·3 RIGHT signposted Leez Priory & Rayne. **Cycle 0·8m to left turn by grass triangle signposted Felsted.**

12·1 LEFT at grass triangle signposted Felsted & Rayne. **Cycle 0·7m to T junction end.**

12·8 LEFT at T junction signposted Felsted & Dunmow. **Cycle 0·3m to right turn signposted Mole Hill Green.**

13·1 RIGHT into Hollow Road signposted Mole Hill Green. **Cycle 0·8m to T junction end.**

13·9 LEFT at T junction signposted Felsted. **Cycle 0·1m to T junction end.**

14·0 RIGHT at T junction signposted Rayne & Braintree. **Cycle 0·3m to right turn signposted Great Leighs & Chelmsford.**

14·3 RIGHT signposted Great Leighs & Chelmsford. **Cycle 0·2m to T junction end.**

14·5 RIGHT at T junction signposted Great Leighs & Chelmsford. **Cycle 1·3m to left turn into County Show Ground.**

15·8 LEFT into Essex County Show Ground.

End of 16m route.

ESSEX - 29M ROUTE

0·0   RIGHT   out of show ground entrance from the same entrance you came in at. **Cycle 0·3m to left turn signposted Littley Green.**

0·3   LEFT   into Hornells Corner signposted Littley Green. **Cycle 0·7m to staggered crossroads end.**

The 59m route turns left here, you continue.

1·0   CONT   over staggered crossroads signposted Littley Green into Howe Street. **Cycle 2·0m to left turn by grass triangle signposted Old Shaws.**

2·6   Compasses Inn.

3·0   LEFT   signposted Old Shaws. **Cycle 0·2m to small unsignposted T junction.**

3·2   RIGHT   at small unsignposted T junction. **Cycle 0·3m to small unsignposted T junction.**

3·5   RIGHT   at small unsignposted T junction. **Cycle 1·1m to T junction end.**

4·6   LEFT   at T junction signposted Howe Street & Little Walthams. **Cycle 0·2m to T junction end.**

4·8   RIGHT   at T junction signposted Howe Street & The Walthams. **Cycle 0·1m to T junction end.**

4·9   RIGHT   at T junction signposted Howe Street & Pleshey. **Cycle 0·3m to T junction end.**

5·2   LEFT   at unsignposted T junction. **Cycle 0·3m to right turn signposted Pleshey 2.**

5·5   RIGHT   signposted Pleshey 2. **Cycle 0·3m to left turn signposted The Chignalls &Mashbury.**

5·8   *The 15m route continues, you turn left.*

5·8   LEFT   signposted The Chignalls &Mashbury. **Cycle 0·4m to T junction end.**

6·0 CONT through ford.

6·2 RIGHT at T junction signposted The Chignalls & Mashbury.
Cycle 0·3m to unsignposted left turn.

6·5 LEFT unsignposted. **Cycle 0·4m to grass triangle and
T junction end.**

6·9 RIGHT at grass triangle and T junction signposted The
Chignalls. **Cycle 1·2m to T junction end.**

8·1 RIGHT at T junction into Chignall Road signposted Chignall
Smealy. **Cycle 1·2m to T junction end.**

9·3 RIGHT at T junction signpostedMashbury & The Easters.
Cycle 1·5m to left turn signposted Good Easter.

10·7 *For a food stop and a good PH (The Fox) turn
right signposted Waltham and cycle 0·2m returning
here afterwards to continue with route.*

10·8 LEFT signposted Good Easter & The Rodings.
**Cycle 1·6m to right turn signposted Pleshey &
The Walthams.**

12·4 The Star PH.

12·4 RIGHT signposted Pleshey & The Walthams. **Cycle 0·9m to
grass triangle and T junction end.**

13·3 RIGHT at grass triangle and T junction signposted Mashbury
& Pleshey. **Cycle 0·9m to grass triangle and T
junction end.**

14·2 LEFT at grass triangle and T junction signposted Pleshey &
High Easter. **Cycle 2·9m to right turn signposted
Pentlowend & High Roding, by The PunchBowl
Inn.**

17·1 The Punch Bowl and The Cork & Bell Inns.

17·1 RIGHT by Punch Bowl signposted Pentlowend & High
Roding. **Cycle 0·7m to T junction end.**

17·8 RIGHT at T junction signposted High Roding.
Cycle 1·0m to T junction end.

18·8 LEFT at T junction signposted Dunmow. **Cycle 0·2m to
right turn signposted Pleshey.**

19·0 RIGHT signposted Pleshey. **Cycle 2·9m to staggered
crossroads end.
Ignore any future signposts for Pleshey.**

21·9 CONT over staggered crossroads with A130 (right then left)
signposted North End into Bennetts Lane. **Cycle 2m
to T junction end.**

23·9 RIGHT at T junction signposted Braintree. **Cycle 0·1m to
right turn signposted Chelmsford B1417.**

24·0 RIGHT signposted Chelmsford into Chelmsford Road. **Cycle
0·6m to left turn signposted Coblers Green.**

24·6 LEFT signposted Coblers Green. **Cycle 1·1m to
T junction end.**

25·7 RIGHT at T junction signposted Great. Leighs. **Cycle 0·3m to
left turn signpostedMole Hill Green.**

26·0 LEFT into Hollow Road signpostedMole Hill Green.
Cycle 0·8m to T junction end.

26·8 LEFT at T junction signposted Flestead.
Cycle 0·1m to T junction end.

26·9 RIGHT at T junction signposted Rayne & Braintree. **Cycle
0·3m to right turn signposted Great Leighs.**

27·2 RIGHT signposted Great Leighs & Chelmsford.
Cycle 0·2m to T junction end.

27·4 RIGHT at T junction signposted Great Leighs & Chelmsford.
Cycle 1·3m to left turn into Show Ground.

28·7 LEFT into Essex County Show Ground.

End of 29m route.

ESSEX - 58 MILE ROUTE

0·0   RIGHT   out of show ground entrance from the same entrance you came in at. **Cycle 0·3m to left turn signposted Littley Green.**

0·3   LEFT   into Hornells Corner signposted Littley Green. **Cycle 0·7m to T junction end.**

1·0   *The shorter routes turn right here, you turn left.*

1·0   LEFT   at T junction signposted Great Leighs. **Cycle 1m to staggered crossroads end.**

2·0   CONT   over staggered crossroads with A131 (right then left) signposted Great Leighs Church into Borham Road. **Cycle 1·0m to left turn signposted Fuller Street.**

2·0   The St. Anne's Castle Inn.

3·0   LEFT   signposted Fuller Street. **Cycle 2·6m to left turn signposted Hatfield Peverel.**

3·6   The Square & Compasses Inn.

5·5   The Raleigh Arms PH.

5·6   LEFT   signposted Hatfield Peverel. **Cycle 2·6m to T junction end.**

8·2   RIGHT   at unsignposted T junction end. **Cycle 0·1m to first left turn signposted Peverels.**

8·3   LEFT   into Church Street signposted Peverels. **Cycle 0·2m to right turn into Crabb's Hill.**

8·5   RIGHT   into Crabb's Hill. **Cycle 0·9m to right turn signposted Boreham.**

9·4   RIGHT   signposted Boreham. **Cycle 0·5m to T junction.**

9·9   LEFT   signposted Little Baddow. **Cycle 3·2m to mini roundabout end.**

10·3   The Rodney Inn.

11·8 The Generals Arms PH.

13·1 RIGHT at mini roundabout signposted Chelmsford A414, then left turn at immediate second mini roundabout into Mayes Lane. **Cycle 0·3m to right turn signposted Sandon.**

13·4 RIGHT into Penny Royal Road signposted Sandon. **Cycle 0·2m to T junction end.**

3·6 RIGHT signposted Sandon. **Cycle 0·7m to unsignposted left turn by phone box .**

14·3 LEFT unsignposted by phone box. **Cycle 0·6m to T junction end.**

14·9 RIGHT at unsignposted T junction. **Cycle 0·8m to T junction end.**

15·7 LEFT at T junction signposted Butts Green. **Cycle 0·6m to T junction end.**

16·3 LEFT at T junction signposted East Hanningford. **Cycle 3·5m to staggered crossroads end.**

17·5 The Three Horseshoes PH.

19·8 The Bell PH.

19·8 CONT over staggered crossroads with A130 (right then left)signposted Hanningford. **Cycle 2·3m to T junction end.**

22·1 RIGHT at T junction into Hawkswood Road signposted Stock. **Cycle 1·8m to right turn signposted Stock.**

23·9 RIGHT into Downham Road signposted Stock. **Cycle 0·6m to left turn signposted stock.**

24·5 LEFT into Mill Road signposted Stock. **Cycle 0·7m to unsignposted left turn into Well Lane.**

25·2 LEFT at unsignposted crossroads into Well lane. **Cycle 1·2m to T junction end with B1007.**

26·4   RIGHT   at unsignposted T junction by Old Kings Head PH. **Cycle 0·2m to left turn signposted Ingatestone.**

26·6   LEFT   into Ingatestone Road signposted Ingatestone. **Cycle 2·7m to crossroads with B1002.**

29·3   CONT   over crossroads with Ingatestone High Street into Fryerning Lane. **Cycle 0·8m T junction end.**

30·1   RIGHT   at T junction opposite Woolpack PH signposted Highwood. **Cycle 2·6m to T junction end.**

31·2   The Viper PH.

31·6   The Cricketers PH.

32·7   LEFT   at T junction into Blackmore Road signposted Blackmore. **Cycle 1·9m to right turn into Spriggs Lane.**

34·6   RIGHT   into Spriggs Lane. **Cycle 0·9m to T junction end.**

35·5   RIGHT   at unsignposted T junction into Fingrith Hall Lane. **Cycle 0·7m to staggered crossroads end.**

36·2   CONT   over staggered crossroads with A414 (turn left and cycle 0·1m to right turn) signposted Norton Heath. **Cycle 0·3m to left turn signposted Willingale.**

36·6   LEFT   signposted Willingale. **Cycle 2·1m to T junction.**

Norton Heath Cafe.

38·7   LEFT   signposted Willingale. **Cycle 1·2m to right turn signposted Roxwell.**

39·1   RIGHT   signposted Roxwell. **Cycle 0·5m to left turn signposted Birds Green.**

40·4   LEFT   signposted Birds Green. **Cycle 0·9m to right turn signposted Berners Roding.**

41·3   RIGHT   signposted Berners Roding. **Cycle 2·2m to staggered crossroads end with A1060.**

44·3 CONT over unsignposted staggered crossroads with A1060 (left then right). **Cycle 1·4m to right turn signposted High Easter.**

44·9 RIGHT signposted High Easter. **Cycle 0·6m to T junction.**

45·5 LEFT at T junction signposted High Easter. **Cycle 0·9m to left turn by signposted High Roding.**

46·4 Cork and Bell PH.

46·4 LEFT signposted High Roding. **Cycle 0·7m to T junction.**

47·1 RIGHT at T junction signposted High Roding. **Cycle 1·0m to T junction end.**

48·1 LEFT at T junction signposted Dunmow. **Cycle 0·2m to right turn signposted Pleshey.**

48·3 RIGHT signposted Pleshey. **Cycle 2·9m to staggered crossroads end. Ignore any future signs for Pleshey.**

51·2 CONT over staggered crossroads with A130 (right then left) signposted North End into Bennetts Lane. **Cycle 2·0m to T junction end.**

53·2 RIGHT at T junction signposted Braintree. **Cycle 0·1m to right turn signposted Chelmsford B1417.**

53·3 RIGHT at B1417 signposted Chelmsford into Chelmsford Road. **Cycle 0·6m to left turn signposted Coblers Green.**

53·3 Swan Hotel.

53·9 Yew Tree PH.

53·9 LEFT signposted Coblers Green. **Cycle 1·1m to T junction end.**

55·0 RIGHT at T junction signposted Great Leighs. **Cycle 0·3m to left turn signposted Mole Hill Green.**

55·3 LEFT   into Hollow Road signposted Mole Hill Green.
              Cycle 0·8m to T junction end.

56·1 LEFT   at T junction signposted Felsted.
              Cycle 0·1m to T junction end.

56·2 RIGHT   at T junction signposted Rayne & Braintree.
              Cycle 0·3m to right turn signposted Great Leighs.

56·5 RIGHT   signposted Great Leighs & Chelmsford.
              Cycle 0·2m to T junction end.

56·7 RIGHT   at T junction signposted Great Leighs & Chelmsford.
              Cycle 1·3m to left turn into Show ground.

58·0 LEFT   into Essex County Show Ground.

              End of 58m route.

OFF THE BEATEN TRACK IN RURAL HAMPSHIRE

The authors' home County and the cycling routes which inspired them to start Bike 1. The rides start and finish in Fleet and venture into the peaceful and unspoilt country lanes of Hampshire.

The 17m route is fairly flat and makes for easy going through Crookham and Odiham. The 22m ride goes through Crondall and Lower Froyle on leafy rolling lanes and returns to Fleet via Odiham. Choose the 53m route and you'll enjoy a varied and challenging cycle ride. It is fairly flat, up until where the 22m route turns off, then follows quiet lanes to Selborne - once the home of Gilbert White. From here there is a stiff climb to the hill-top past Goleigh Farm. The going eases with some undulating sections to follow, with the attraction of a refreshment stop at *The Pub With No Name*, at the half way point.

All three routes return to Fleet via the back roads of Odiham Common. This whole area is a patchwork of minor roads and lanes, so it is easy to extend or shorten the routes to suit your motivation on the day.

Map	OS LR 186 Aldershot & Guildford.
Distance	17, 22 or 53 miles.
Start/Finish	Church of Our Lady Hall, Kings Road, Fleet.

Railway Access

Fleet - start of the route, trains from London Waterloo.

Farnham - 2.5m east of the route, trains from Waterloo.

Alton - centre of the long route, trains from Waterloo.

Places to see

Fleet Pond. A nature reserve which is Hampshire's largest freshwater lake. Well over 1000 species live in or visit the reserve.

Selborne Hill. The wooded slopes rise steeply above Selborne.

Selborne. The home of Gilbert White, naturalist and author of *'The Natural History of Selborne'*.

Gilbert White's House & The Oates Museum, The Wakes, Selborne. White's 18th century home and gardens containing original manuscripts and beautifully furnished rooms. The Oates Musem celebrates the lives of Frank Oates, the Victorian explorer, and Captain Lawrence Oates, the tragic hero of Scott's Antarctic Expedition.

Tourist Information Office, Gurkha Square, Fleet 0252 811151.

Refreshments

The George PH & shops, Odiham - 9.3m, 15.4m, 46.4m.

Red Lion PH, Oakhanger - 17.4m, 53m route.

Selborne Arms PH, 20·7m, 53m route.

Pub With No Name, just off ride - 26.5m, 53m route.

HAMPSHIRE
OFF THE BEATEN TRACK IN RURAL HAMPSHIRE

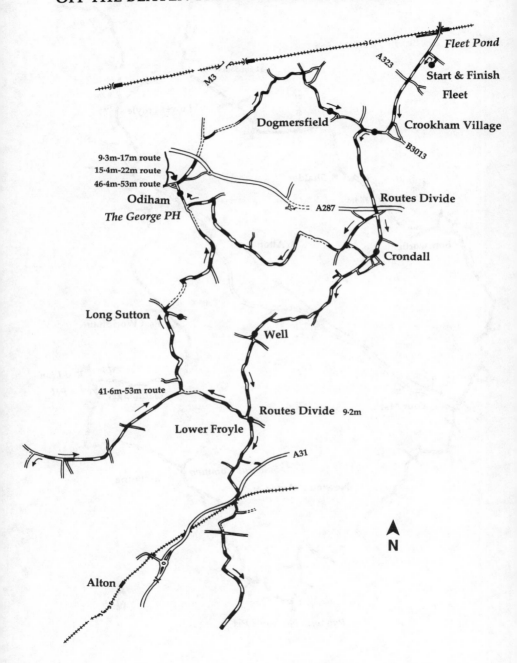

Fleet Pond

A323

Start & Finish

Fleet

Dogmersfield

Crookham Village

B3013

9·3m-17m route
15·4m-22m route
46·4m-53m route

Odiham
The George PH

Routes Divide

A287

Crondall

Long Sutton

Well

41·6m-53m route

Routes Divide   9·2m

Lower Froyle

A31

Alton

N

HAMPSHIRE
OFF THE BEATEN TRACK IN RURAL HAMPSHIRE

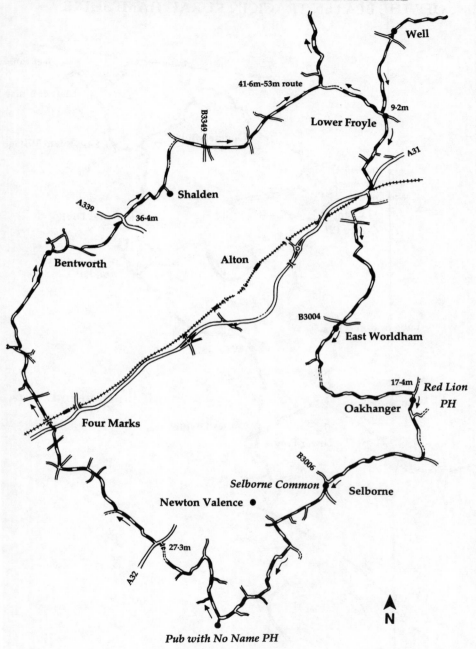

Well

41·6m–53m route

B3349

9·2m

Lower Froyle

A31

A339

Shalden

36·4m

Bentworth

Alton

B3004

East Worldham

17·4m

Red Lion PH

Four Marks

Oakhanger

B3006

Selborne Common

Selborne

Newton Valence

27·3m

A32

N

Pub with No Name PH

HAMPSHIRE - 17M ROUTE

0·0 **LEFT** out of Our Lady Church Hall. **Cycle 0·1m to second set of traffic lights**.

0·1 **LEFT** at traffic lights to Fleet Road. **Cycle 0·6m to major crossroads by Oatsheaf PH.**

0·7 **CONT** at crossroads by Oatsheaf PH into Crookham Road. **Cycle 1·1m to T junction end.**

1·8 **RIGHT** at T junction into the street signposted Crookham. **Cycle 0·5m to left turn signposted Crondall 2 ½.**

2·3 **LEFT** signposted Crondall 2 ½. **Cycle 1·6m to T junction end.**

3·9 **CONT** over busy T junction (A287) onto footpath ahead. **Cycle 0·6m to the end of the path.**

4·1 **RIGHT** at end of path signposted Odiham 4m (this signpost is behind you). **Cycle 0·4m to first left turn signposted Itchel.**

The 22m & 53m routes go straight ahead here.

4·5 **LEFT** signposted Itchel. **Cycle 0·3m to T junction end.**

4·8 **RIGHT** at T junction signposted The Pit. Beware of sharp left bend in 1m. **Cycle 2·3m to Roke Farm.**

7·1 **CONT** through Roke Farm (not on footpath). **Cycle 1·3m to T junction end.**

8·4 **LEFT** at unsignposted T junction. **Cycle 0·4m to T junction end.**

8·8 **RIGHT** at unsignposted T junction. **Cycle 0·5m to T junction in Odiham.**

9·3 **RIGHT** at T junction into Odiham High Street. **Cycle 0·1m to left turn signposted The Vine Church.**

9·4 **LEFT** signposted The Vine Church. **Cycle 0·4m to**

footpath end by bottlebanks.

9·9   RIGHT   onto footpath by bottlebank and under the bridge. **Cycle 0·1m to end by cattle grid.**

10·0   RIGHT   onto unsignposted road over cattlegrid. **Cycle 0·3m to first right into Bagwell Lane.**

10·3   RIGHT   into Bagwell Lane. **Cycle 1·8m to T junction end.**

12·2   RIGHT   at grass triangle signposted Dogmersfield. **Cycle 2·3m to left turn signposted Fleet 1 ¼.**

15·7   LEFT   signposted Fleet 1 ¼ & Crookham Road. **Cycle 0·9m to traffic lights and crossroads in Fleet.**

16·6   CONT   through traffic lights. **Cycle 0·6m to right turn & traffic lights signposted Aldershot into Kings Road.**

17·2   RIGHT   into Kings Road signposted Aldershot A323. **Cycle 0·1m to Church of Our Lady Hall on right.**

17·3   RIGHT   into Church of Our Lady church hall.

End of 17m route.

HAMPSHIRE - 22 MILE ROUTE

0·0   **LEFT**   out of Church Hall onto Kings Road. **Cycle 0·1m to second set of traffic lights with T junction.**

0·1   **LEFT**   at T junction & traffic light onto Fleet Road. **Cycle 0·6m down High Street to crossroads & traffic lights by Oatsheaf PH.**

0·7   **CONT**   at crossroads & traffic lights and Oatsheaf PH into Crookham Road. **Cycle 1·1m to T junction end.**

1·8   **RIGHT**   at T junction into The Street. **Cycle 0·5m to left turn signposted Crondall 2 ½.**

2·3   **LEFT**   signposted Crondall 2 ½. **Cycle 1·6m to T junction end.**

3·9   **CONT**   over busy T junction with A287 onto footpath ahead. **Cycle 0·1m to end of path.**

4·0   **CONT**   at T junction signposted Well 3 ½. **Cycle 3·5m through Crondall Village to crossroads by a well.**

The 15m route turns right here.

7·7   **CONT**   at crossroads by well signposted Froyle 1 ½ & Single Track Road. **Cycle 1·5m to T junction end.**

The 53m route turns left here.

9·2   **RIGHT**   at T junction in front of Prince of Wales PH. **Cycle 1·3m to right turn signposted Long Sutton 1 ½.**

10·5   **RIGHT**   signposted Long Sutton 1 ½. **Cycle 1·6m to T junction end.**

12·2   **LEFT**   at T junction by duck pond. **Cycle 0·1m to immediate unsignposted first right turn.**

12·3   **RIGHT**   into unsignposted road by telegraph pole. **Cycle 1·3m to T junction end.**

13·6   **LEFT**   at T junction & onto unsignposted road. **Cycle 1·8m** to T junction in Odiham village.

15·4   RIGHT   at T junction signposted Car Park. **Cycle 0·1m to first left turn signposted The Vine Church.**

15·5   LEFT   signposted The Vine Church. **Cycle 0·4m to footpath end by bottlebanks.**

16·0   RIGHT   onto footpath by bottlebank and under the bridge. **Cycle 0·1m to end by cattle grid.**

16·1   RIGHT   onto unsignposted road over cattlegrid. **Cycle 0·3m to first right.**

16·4   RIGHT   into Bagwell Lane. **Cycle 1·8m to T junction end.**

18·2   RIGHT   at grass triangle signposted Dogmersfield. **Cycle 2·3m to a left turn signposted Fleet 1 ¼.**

20·7   LEFT   signposted Fleet 1 ¼ & Crookham Road. **Cycle 0·9m to crossroads and traffic lights in Fleet.**

21·6   CONT   over crossroads and traffic lights. **Cycle 0·6m to traffic lights & right turn to Kings Road, signposted Aldershot A323**

22·2   RIGHT   into Kings Road signposted Aldershot A323. **Cycle 0·1m to Church of Our Lady Hall on the right.**

22·3   RIGHT   into Church Hall.

End of 22m route.

HAMPSHIRE - 53 MILE ROUTE

0·0 LEFT out of Church Hall onto Kings Road. **Cycle 0·1m to 2nd set of traffic lights with T junction.**

0·1 LEFT at T junction & traffic light onto Fleet Road. **Cycle 0·6m down High Street to crossroads and traffic lights by Oatsheaf PH.**

0·7 CONT at crossroads and Oatsheaf PH into Crookham Road. **Cycle 1·1m to T junction end.**

1·8 RIGHT at T junction into The Street. **Cycle 0·5m to left turn signposted Crondall 2 ½.**

2·3 LEFT signposted Crondall 2 ½. **Cycle 1·6m to T junction end.**

3·9 CONT over busy T junction with A287 onto footpath ahead. **Cycle 0·1m to end of path.**

4·0 CONT at T junction signposted Well 3½. **Cycle 3·5m through Crondall Village to crossroads by a well.**

The 17m route turns right here.

7·7 CONT at crossroads by well, signposted Froyle 1 ½ & Single Track Road. **Cycle 1·5m to T junction end.**

9·2 LEFT at T junction in front of Prince of Wales PH. **Cycle to immediate right turn signposted Upper Froyle 1.**

The 22m route turns right here.

9·3 RIGHT signposted Upper Froyle 1. **Cycle 1·4m to dual carriageway T junction end.**

10·7 RIGHT onto dual carriageway signposted A31 - **Caution! Cycle 0·2m to first left signposted Mill Court ¼.**

10·9 LEFT signpostedMill Court. **Cycle 0·8m to crossroads end.**

11·7 CONT over crossroads signposted Wyke. **Cycle 2·4m to T junction end.**

14·1 RIGHT at T junction signposted B3004. **Cycle 0·1m to first left signposted West Worldham in front of Three Horseshoes PH.**

14·2 LEFT signposted West Worldham. **Cycle 1m to left turn by grass triangle signposted Hartley Church.**

15·0 LEFT at grass triangle signposted Hartley Church. **Cycle 2·4m to T junction end.**

17·4 RIGHT at T junction & Red Lion PH signposted Selbourne. **Cycle 1·3m to T junction end with grass triangle.**

18·7 RIGHT at T junction with grass triangle signposted Selbourne 2. **Cycle 2m to T junction end.**

20·7 LEFT at T junction signposted B3006. **Cycle 0·1m to first right signposted Newton Valance.**

20·8 RIGHT signposted Newton Valance 1 ¾. **Cycle 1·2m to left turn signposted Hawkley 2.**

22·0 LEFT at grass triangle signposted Hawkley 2. **Cycle 0·3m to first right.**

22·3 RIGHT signposted Priors Dean 1 ¼. **Cycle 1m to T junction with small grass triangle.**

23·3 RIGHT at unsignposted T junction with grass triangle. **Cycle 1·9m to T junction end.**

24·7 RIGHT at T junction signposted Colemore. **Cycle 1·3m to T junction end.**

For an interesting PH turn left here and first left up a track to 'The Pub With No Name'.

26·0 LEFT at unsignposted T junction. **Cycle 0·5m to first right turn signposted Farringdon 3 ¾.**

26·5 RIGHT signposted Farringdon 3 ¾. **Cycle 0·8m to T junction end with A32.**

27·3 LEFT at unsignposted T junction. **Cycle 0·1m to immediate right turn by red brick house.**

27·4 RIGHT into unsignposted road near red brick house. **Cycle 0·9m to right turn signposted Four Marks.**

28·3 RIGHT signposted Four Marks. **Cycle 1·6m to T junction end with A31.**

29·9 CONT over staggered crossroads with A31 and into Lyminton Bottom Road. **Cycle 2·5m to T junction.**

32·4 LEFT at T junction into High Street Road. **Cycle 0·1m to first right signposted Lasham.**

32·5 RIGHT signposted Lasham. **Cycle 2·3m to roundabout.**

34·8 RIGHT at roundabout past Star Inn signposted Lasham. **Cycle 0·3m to first right signposted Shalden 2 ¼.**

35·1 RIGHT signposted Shalden 2 ¼. **Cycle 1·3m to T junction.**

36·4 LEFT at T junction signposted A339. **Cycle 0·1m to first right signposted Shalden 1.**

36·5 RIGHT signposted Shalden 1. **Cycle 2m to T junction end.**

38·5 RIGHT signposted Alton 3 ½. **Cycle 0·5m to crossroads.**

39·0 CONT over crossroads signposted Froyle 3 ½. **Cycle 2·7m to left turn signposted Long Sutton 1 ½.**

41·6 LEFT signposted Long Sutton 1 ½. **Cycle 1·6m to T junction end.**

43·2 LEFT at T junction by duck pond. **Cycle 0·1m to immediate unsignposted first right turn.**

43·3 RIGHT into unsignposted road. **Cycle 1·3m to T junction.**

44·6 LEFT at unsignposted T junction. **Cycle 1·8m to T junction in Odiham village.**

46·4 RIGHT at T junction signposted Car Park. **Cycle 0·1m to first left turn signposted The Vine Church.**

46·6 LEFT signposted The Vine Church. **Cycle 0·4m to footpath end by bottlebank.**

47·0 RIGHT onto footpath by bottlebank and under the bridge. **Cycle 0·1m to end by cattle grid.**

47·1 RIGHT over cattlegrid onto unsignposted road. **Cycle 0·3m to first right into Bagwell Lane.**

47·4 RIGHT into Bagwell Lane. **Cycle 1·8m to T junction end.**

49·2 RIGHT at grass triangle signposted Dogmersfield. **Cycle 2·3m to a left turn signposted Fleet 1 ¼.**

51·1 LEFT signposted Fleet 1 ¼ & Crookham Road. **Cycle 0·9m to traffic lights and crossroads in Fleet.**

52·4 CONT through traffic lights. **Cycle 0·6m to traffic lights with right turn signposted Aldershot A323.**

53·0 RIGHT into Kings Road signposted Aldershot A323. **Cycle 0·1m to Church of Our Lady Hall on right.**

53·1 RIGHT into Church of Our Lady church hall.

End of 53m route.

HILLS, HOPS, ORCHARDS & MARSH

This Ride starts and finishes at Charing Railway Station. It could just as easily be started at Ashford, Wye or Pluckley railway stations. All three routes start by heading east, parallel to the North Downs Way, to Westwell, where the 18 mile route heads back to Charing via Pluckley.

The longer routes head east to cross the Great Stour river at the charming village of Wye, with its impressive college. There follows a hilly section with a nice climb over the North Downs at Brabourne, just before the longer routes divide at Brabourne Lees. The 45m route skirts south of Ashford to return to Charing.

The 71 mile route continues south, over the Royal Military Canal to Romney Marsh and the Kent coast. The land is flat and open and makes for excellent cycling. After 35 miles the seaside village of Dymchurch is reached - an ideal place to stop for lunch. On leaving the Marsh the ride uses classic country lanes to pass through the farming areas south-west of Ashford before heading past the orchards to the north-west back to Charing.

Map	OS LR 189 Ashford and Romney Marsh.
Distance	18, 45 or 70 miles.
Start/Finish	Charing Railway Station.

Railway Access

Charing, Ashford & Pluckley - trains from London Charing Cross.

Places to see

Pluckley. A charming village famous for being the location for the TV series 'The Darling Buds of May'. It is also reputed to be the most haunted village in Kent, if not Britain!

Eastwell Park, Ashford. A historic 3000 acre estate north of Ashford.

Westwell. Attractive village with many interesting buildings, including *The Mill*, a private house complete with water wheel, and a 13th century church.

Wye. Mediaeval buildings of Wye College.

Museum of Agriculture, Wye. Housed in a fine 14th Century tithe barn. Includes displays of traditional hop cultivation in a Kent Oast House.

Rare Breeds Centre, Woodchurch. 90 acres and 65 species of rare farm animals at Highlands Farm, off the B2067 near Woodchurch.

Woodchurch Windmill. A perfectly restored Kentish Smock Mill.

Dymchurch. See the sea, Martello towers built in 1804 as defences against Napoleonic invasion and take a trip on the Romney Hythe and Dymchurch railway - the world's smallest public railway.

Tourist Information Office, The Churchyard, Ashford 0233 629165.

Refreshments

Tickled Trout PH, Wye - 8.8m, 45m & 70m routes.

Friars Arms PH, Mersham- 27.7m, 45m route.

Pubs, shops & cafes, Dymchurch - 35.4m, 70m route.

Woolpack Inn, near Woodchurch - 44.3m, 70m route.

HILLS, HOPS, ORCHARDS & MARSH

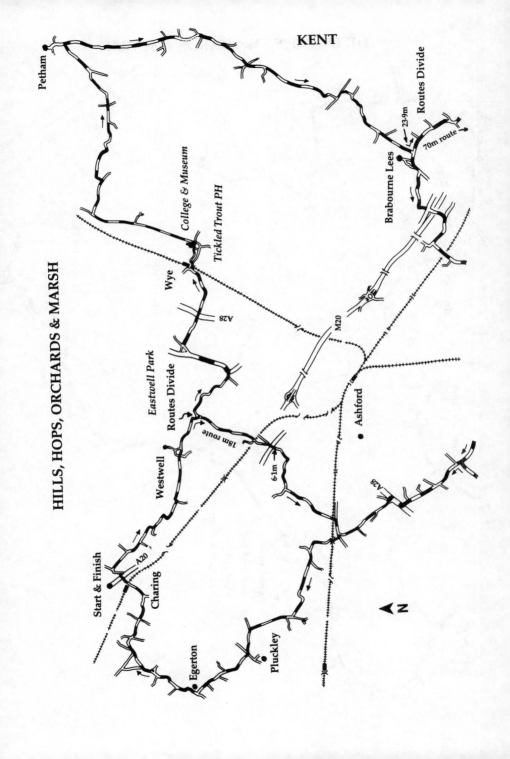

KENT

Petham

College & Museum
Tickled Trout PH
Wye
A28
Eastwell Park
Routes Divide
Westwell
18m route
Start & Finish
Charing
A20
Egerton
Pluckley
6·1m
Ashford
M20
Brabourne Lees
23·9m
Routes Divide
70m route
A28

N

HILLS, HOPS, ORCHARDS & MARSH

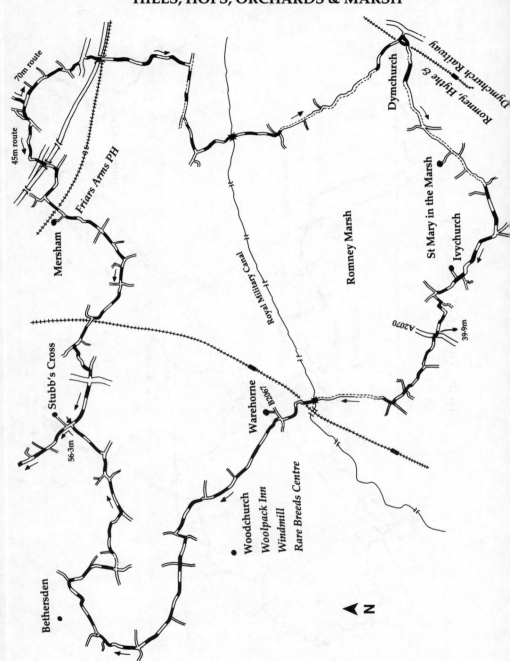

70m route

45m route

Friars Arms PH

Mersham

Stubb's Cross

56·3m

Bethersden

Woodchurch
Woolpack Inn
Windmill
Rare Breeds Centre

Warehorne

B2067

Royal Military Canal

Romney Marsh

Dymchurch

Romney, Hythe &
Dymchurch Railway

St Mary in the Marsh

Ivychurch

A2070

39·9m

N

KENT - 18M ROUTE

0·0   LEFT   out of station. **Cycle 0·3m to crossroads end.**

0·3   CONT   over crossroads signposted Charing. **Cycle 0·2m to right turn signposted Westwell into Pett Lane.**

0·5   RIGHT   signposted Westwell into Pett Lane. **Cycle 0·8m to unsignposted left turn.**

0·3   LEFT   unsignposted. **Cycle 1·3m to T junction with grass triangle.**

2·6   LEFT   at T junction with grass triangle signposted Westwell. **Cycle 0·9m to T junction end.**

3·5   LEFT   at T junction onto main road signposted Kennington, Boughton Lees 3 & Wye 5. **Cycle 0·9m to right turn signposted Potters Corner 1 ½.**

3·5   The Wheel Inn.

4·4   RIGHT   signposted Potters Corner 1 ½. **Cycle 1·2m to T junction end.**

The longer routes continue here.

5·6   LEFT   at unsignposted T junction. **Cycle 0·1m to T junction end.**

5·7   RIGHT   at T junction signposted Godinton ¾ & Ashford 2. **Cycle 0·4m to crossroads end with A20.**

6·1   CONT   over crossroads signposted Godinton ¾ into Godinton Lane. **Cycle 2·3m to T junction end.**

6·1   The Hare and Hounds PH.

8·4   RIGHT   at T junction signposted Bethersden & Tenterden. **Cycle 1·1m to T junction end.**

9·5   LEFT   at T junction signposted Bethersden & Pluckley. **Cycle 1·5m to T junction end.**

11·0   RIGHT   at T junction signposted Little Chart & Pluckley.

Cycle 0·9m to T junction end.

11·9 LEFT at T junction signposted Pluckley & Smarden.
Cycle 0·5m to staggered crossroads end.

12·4 CONT over staggered crossroads signposted Egerton 1 ¾.
Cycle 1·8m to T junction in Egerton.

14·2 RIGHT at T junction in Egerton signposted Charing Heath
1 ¾ & Charing 3 ¾. **Cycle 1·4m to left turn
signposted Lenham 3 & Maidstone 13.**

15·6 LEFT signposted Lenham 3 & Maidstone 5.
Cycle 0·5m to T junction end.

16·1 RIGHT signposted Charing 2 ¾. **Cycle 0·5m to T junction.**

16·6 LEFT at T junction signposted Charing 2 & Ashford 8.
Cycle 1·3m to T junction end.

17·9 LEFT at T junction signposted Charing. **Cycle 0·4m to a
left turn into Charing Station before crossroads.**

18·3 LEFT into Charing Station.

End of 18m route.

KENT - 45 MILE ROUTE

0·0   LEFT   out of station. **Cycle 0·3m to crossroads end.**

0·3   CONT   over crossroads signposted Charing. **Cycle 0·2m to right turn signposted Westwell into Pett Lane.**

0·5   RIGHT   signposted Westwell into Pett Lane. **Cycle 0·8m to unsignposted left turn.**

1·3   LEFT   unsignposted. **Cycle 1·3m to T junction with grass triangle.**

2·6   LEFT   at T junction with grass triangle signposted Westwell. **Cycle 0·9m to T junction end.**

3·5   LEFT   at T junction onto main road signposted Kennington, Boughton Lees 3 & Wye 5. **Cycle 2·2m to T junction end.**

4·4   *The 18m route turns right here.*

5·7   LEFT   at T junction signposted Boughton Aluph, Challock & Ashford. **Cycle 0·1m to T junction end.**

5·8   LEFT   at T junction signposted Challock, Faversham A251 & Broughton Lees ½. **Cycle 0·9m to first right turn opposite St Christopher's Church.**

6·7   RIGHT   unsignposted opposite St Christopher's Church. **Cycle 0·1m to T junction end.**

6·8   RIGHT   at unsignposted T junction. **Cycle 1m to crossroads end with A28.**

7·8   CONT   over crossroads into Harville Road signposted Wye, Brook & Hastingleigh. **Cycle 0·9m to T junction.**

8·7   RIGHT   at T junction signposted Brook 3 & Hastingleigh 4. **Cycle 0·1m to first left signposted Free Parking.**

8·8   The Tickled Trout PH.

8·8   LEFT   signposted Free Parking into Churchfield Road.

Cycle 0·4m to left turn signposted Crundale 3.

9·2   LEFT   signposted Crundale 3 into Olantigh Road.
Cycle 2·2m to right signposted Crundale 1 ½.

11·4   RIGHT   signposted Crundale 1 ½ & Waltham 3. **Cycle 0·7m to left turn signposted Sole Street 1 ¾.**

12·1   LEFT   signposted Sole Street 1 ¾ & Waltham 2 ½.
Cycle 1·8m to crossroads end.

13·7   The Compasses Inn.

13·9   CONT   over crossroads signposted Avil Green & Petham.
Cycle 1·0m to T junction end.

14·9   LEFT   at T junction signposted Petham & Canterbury.
Cycle 1·3m to right turn signposted Elmstead 4.

16·2   RIGHT   signposted Elmstead 4 & Evington 4.
Cycle 3·2m to T junction with grass triangle.

19·4   RIGHT   at T junction with grass triangle signposted Elmstead, Hastingleigh & Wye. **Cycle 1·3m to left turn signposted Brabourne.**

20·7   LEFT   signposted Brabourne. **Cycle 2m to T junction.**

22·7   LEFT   at unsignposted T junction into Brabourne.
Cycle 0·2m to first unsignposted right turn.

22·9   RIGHT   unsignposted. **Cycle 0·2m to T junction with grass triangle.**

23·1   RIGHT   at T junction signposted Smeeth 2 ¾ & Ashford 7 ½.
Cycle 0·8m to T junction end.

23·1   The Five Bells Free House.

23·9   RIGHT   at T junction signposted Smeeth ¾ & Ashford 5.
Cycle 0·3m to T junction end.

The 71m route turns left here.

24·2   LEFT   at T junction signposted Smeeth ½ & Ashford 5.

Cycle 0·2m to right turn signposted Mersham 1 ¾.

24·2   The Woolpack PH.

24·4 RIGHT signposted Mersham 1 ¾ & Ashford 5. **Cycle 0·9m
to crossroads end with A20.**

25·3 CONT over unsignposted crossroads, ignore dead end sign.
Cycle 0·4m to T junction end.

25·7 RIGHT at unsignposted T junction with Grass triangle.
Cycle 0·6m to left turn signposted Aldington.

26·3 LEFT signposted Aldington & Bilsington into Church Road.
Cycle 2·0m to T junction end.

26·7   The Farriers Arms PH.

28·3 RIGHT at T junction signposted Kingsnorth 2 ½ & Ashford 5.
**Cycle 2·1m to unsignposted second left turn
after railway bridge.**

30·4 LEFT unsignposted. **Cycle 0·6m to T junction end.**

31·0 RIGHT at T junction signposted Great Chart & Hothfield 6.
Cycle 0·2m to crossroads end with A2070.

31·2 CONT over crossroads signposted Great Chart into Magpie
Hall Road. **Cycle 2·5m to T junction end.**

33·7 RIGHT at T junction signposted Great Chart. **Cycle 0·2m
to left turn signposted Great Chart & Hothfield 3.**

33·9 LEFT signposted Great Chart & Hothfield 3. **Cycle to
immediate left turn signposted Hothfield.**

33·9 LEFT signposted Hothfield. **Cycle 1·3m to T junction.**

35·2 LEFT at T junction signposted Hothfield, Bethersden &
Tenterden. **Cycle 0·8m to T junction end.**

36·0 LEFT at T junction signposted Bethersden & Pluckley.
Cycle 1·5m to T junction end.

37·5 RIGHT at T junction signposted Little Chart & Pluckley.

Cycle 0·9m to T junction end.

38·4 LEFT at T junction signposted Pluckley & Smarden.
Cycle 0·5m to staggered crossroads end.

38·9 CONT over staggered crossroads signposted Egerton 1 ¾.
Cycle 1·8m to T junction end in Egerton.

40·7 RIGHT at T junction in Egerton signposted Charing Heath
1 ¾ & Charing 3 ¾. **Cycle 1·4m to left turn
signposted Lenham 3 &Maidstone 13.**

42·1 LEFT signposted Lenham 3 & Maidstone 13.
Cycle 0·5m to T junction end.

42·6 RIGHT at T junction signposted Charing 2 ¾.
Cycle 0·5m to T junction end.

43·1 LEFT at T junction signposted Charing 2 & Ashford 8.
Cycle 1·3m to T junction end.

44·4 LEFT at T junction signposted Charing. **Cycle 0·4m to a
left into Charing Station just before busy
crossroads.**

44·8 LEFT into Charing Station.

End of 45m route.

KENT - 70 MILE ROUTE

0·0   LEFT   out of station. **Cycle 0·3m to crossroads end.**

0·3   CONT   over crossroads signposted Charing. **Cycle 0·2m to right turn signposted Westwell into Pett Lane.**

0·5   RIGHT   signposted Westwell into Pett Lane. **Cycle 0·8m to unsignposted left turn.**

1·3   LEFT   unsignposted. **Cycle 1·3m to T junction with grass triangle.**

2·6   LEFT   at T junction with grass triangle signposted Westwell. **Cycle 0·9m to T junction end.**

3·5   LEFT   at T junction onto main road signposted Kennington, Boughton Lees 3 & Wye 5. **Cycle 2·2m to T junction end.**

3·5   The Wheel Inn.

4·4   *The 18m route turns right here.*

5·7   LEFT   at T junction signposted Boughton Aluph, Challock & Ashford. **Cycle 0·1m to T junction end.**

5·8   LEFT   at T junction signposted Challock, Faversham A251 & Broughton Lees ½. **Cycle 0·9m to first right turn opposite St. Christopher's Church.**

6·7   RIGHT   unsignposted, opposite St Christopher's Church. **Cycle 0·1m to T junction end.**

6·8   RIGHT   at unsignposted T junction. **Cycle 1m to crossroads end with A28.**

7·8   CONT   over crossroads into Harville Road signposted Wye, Brook & Hastingleigh. **Cycle 0·9m to T junction.**

8·7   RIGHT   at T junction signposted Brook 3 & Hastingleigh 4. **Cycle 0·1m to first left signposted Free Parking.**

8·8   The Tickled Trout PH.

8·8 LEFT signposted Free Parking into Churchfield Road. **Cycle 0·4m to left turn signposted Crundale 3.**

9·2 LEFT signposted Crundale 3 into Olantigh Road. **Cycle 2·2m to right turn signposted Crundale 1 ½.**

11·4 RIGHT signposted Crundale 1 ½ & Waltham 3. **Cycle 0·7m to left turn signposted Sole Street 1 ¾ & Waltham 2 ½.**

12·1 LEFT signposted Sole Street 1 & Waltham 2. **Cycle 1·8m to crossroads end.**

13·7 The Compasses Inn.

13·9 CONT over crossroads signposted Avil Green & Petham. **Cycle 1·0m to T junction end.**

14·9 LEFT at T junction signposted Petham & Canterbury. **Cycle 1·3m to right turn signposted Elmstead 4.**

16·2 RIGHT signposted Elmstead 4 & Evington 4. **Cycle 3·2m to T junction with grass triangle.**

19·4 RIGHT at T junction with grass triangle signposted Elmstead, Hastingleigh & Wye. **Cycle 1·3m to left turn signposted Brabourne.**

20·7 LEFT signposted Brabourne. **Cycle 2m to T junction.**

22·7 LEFT at unsignposted T junction into Brabourne. **Cycle 0·2m to first unsignposted right turn.**

22·9 RIGHT unsignposted. **Cycle 0·2m to T junction with grass triangle.**

23·1 RIGHT at T junction signposted Smeeth 2 ¾ & Ashford 7 ½. **Cycle 0·8m to T junction end.**

23·1 The Five Bells Free House.

23·9 RIGHT at T junction signposted Smeeth ¾ & Ashford 5. **Cycle 0·3m to T junction end.**

The 45m route turns right here.

24·2 LEFT at T junction signposted Folkestone & Dover A20.
Cycle 0·1m to first unsignposted right turn.

24·3 RIGHT into Harringe Lane. **Cycle 2·1m to T junction.**

26·4 RIGHT at T junction signposted Aldington B2067.
Cycle 1·8m to T junction end.

28·2 LEFT at T junction signposted Dymchurch 5. **Cycle 5·0m
to right turn signposted StMary-in-the-Marsh 2 ½ .**

33·2 RIGHT signposted StMary in theMarsh, Ivychurch 6 & Old
Romney 6 into Mill Road.
Cycle 1·9m to T junction end.

35·1 LEFT at T junction signposted New Romney 2 ¼ & St Mary
Bay 2 ¼. **Cycle 0·1m to first right turn.**

35·2 RIGHT signposted StMary in theMarsh, Old Romney 4 &
Ivychurch 4. **Cycle 2·7m to T junction end.**

35·7 The Star Inn.

37·9 RIGHT at T junction signposted Ivychurch 1, Hamstreet 5 &
Ashford 11. **Cycle 1·8m to left turn signposted
Spring Farm.**

39·1 The Bell Inn.

39·7 LEFT signposted Spring Farm. **Cycle 0·2m to first
unsignposted right turn.**

39·9 RIGHT unsignposted. **Cycle 0·8m to T junction end
with A2070.**

40·7 RIGHT at unsignposted T junction. **Cycle 0·1m to first
unsignposted left turn.**

40·8 LEFT unsignposted. **Cycle 1·2m to crossroads end.**

42·0 CONT over crossroads signposted Warehorne & Snargate.
Cycle 0·4m to T junction end.

42·4 RIGHT at T junction signposted Warehorne 1 ¾.
Cycle 2·4m to crossroads end with B2067.

44·3 The Woolpack Inn.

44·8 CONT over crossroads signposted Bethersden 7 ¾.
Cycle 2·1m to T junction end.

46·9 LEFT at T junction signposted Woodchurch 2 ¼.
Cycle 0·9m to T junction end.

47·8 LEFT at T junction signposted Woodchurch 1 ¼. **Cycle
0·1m to first right turn signposted High Halden 4.**

47·9 RIGHT signposted High Halden 4. **Cycle 0·6m to
crossroads end.**

48·5 CONT over crossroads signposted High Halden.
Cycle 1·8m to crossroads end.

50·3 CONT over crossroads signposted Bethersden 2 ½.
Cycle 0·6m to unsignposted Y shaped junction.

50·9 RIGHT fork at unsignposted shaped junction.
Cycle 1·4m to T junction end.

52·3 RIGHT at T junction signposted Woodchurch 3 & Appledore.
Cycle 0·9m to left turn signposted Shadoxhurst.

53·2 LEFT signposted signposted Shadoxhurst 2 ¼.
Cycle 1·2m to T junction end.

54·4 LEFT at T junction signposted Shadoxhurst & Ashford.
Cycle 1·9m to T junction end.

56·3 LEFT at T junction signposted Great Chart 2 ½ &
Bethersden 5. **Cycle 1·5m to T junction end with
A28.**

57·8 RIGHT at T junction signposted Great Chart. **Cycle 0·2m
to left turn signposted Great Chart & Hothfield 3.**

58·0 LEFT signposted Great Chart & Hothfield 3. **Cycle to
immediate left turn signposted Hothfield.**

58·0 LEFT   signposted Hothfield. **Cycle 1·3m to T junction.**

59·3 LEFT   at T junction signposted Hothfield, Bethersden &
             Tenterden. **Cycle 0·8m to T junction end.**

60·1 LEFT   at T junction signposted Bethersden & Pluckley.
             Cycle 1·5m to T junction end.

61·6 RIGHT   at T junction signposted Little Chart & Pluckley.
             Cycle 0·9m to T junction end.

62·5 LEFT   at T junction signposted Pluckley & Smarden.
             Cycle 0·5m to staggered crossroads end.

63·0 CONT   over staggered crossroads signposted Egerton 1 ¾.
             Cycle 1·8m to T junction end in Egerton.

64·8 RIGHT   at T junction in Egerton signposted Charing Heath
             1 ¾ & Charing 3 ¾. **Cycle 1·4m to left turn
             signposted Lenham 3 &Maidstone 13.**

66·2 LEFT   signposted Lenham 3 &Maidstone 13.
             Cycle 0·5m to T junction end.

66·7 RIGHT   at T junction signposted Charing 2 ¾.
             Cycle 0·5m to T junction end.

67·2 LEFT   at T junction signposted Charing 2 & Ashford 8.
             Cycle 1·3m to T junction end.

68·5 LEFT   signposted Charing. **Cycle 0·4m to left turn into
             Charing Station just before crossroads.**

69·9 LEFT   into Charing Station.

End of 70m route.

PARKS & TOW PATHS

This route does a great job of covering 12 or 20 miles in the south-west suburbs by utilising three parks and the Thames tow path, with a few side roads to link the whole route together. It is a pleasant and easy to follow route but is best avoided on high days and holidays when the motoring fraternity tends to dawdle through Richmond Park gawping at the deer, and the riverside path is heavy with foot traffic.

The 12 mile route starts by going through Bushy Park, then on to Hampton Court Park, along the tow path through Kingston and back to Teddington. The longer route enters Richmond Park through Kingston Gate and takes in a circuit of the largest of London's Royal Parks.

It would be simple to vary the route by leaving Richmond Park at Richmond Gate, on Star & Garter Hill, and continuing back to Teddington alongside the River Thames.

Map	London A to Z is best.
Distance	12 or 20 miles.
Start/Finish	St Frances De Sales Church Hall, Princes Road, Teddington.

Railway Access

Kingston, Hampton Court & Teddington - trains from Waterloo.

Places to see

Hampton Court Palace. Historic Royal Palace built by Wolsey, extended by Henry VIII, with further alterations by Wren.

Bushey Park. Royal deer park with woodland garden.

Richmond Park. One of London's most glorious open spaces.

Ham House. A fine 17th century house, in the hands of the National Trust.

Strawberry Hill House. An imposing 18th century gothic building by Sir Horace Walpole.

Hampton Court. A riverside village adjacent to Bushey Park with many fine 17th century buildings. River boats leave for trips along the Thames.

Tourist Information Office, Old Town Hall, Richmond 081 940 9125.

Refreshments

Tiltyard Cafe, Hampton Court - 5m.

Pubs, cafes & bars, Kingston - 8.3m.

Club Bar, Kingston Rowing Club, where the routes divide - 8.8m.

Leatherby & Christopher Cafe, Richmond Park - 12m.

There is no shortage of refreshment stops off the route in Teddington, Twickenham and Richmond.

MIDDLESEX
PARKS & TOW PATHS

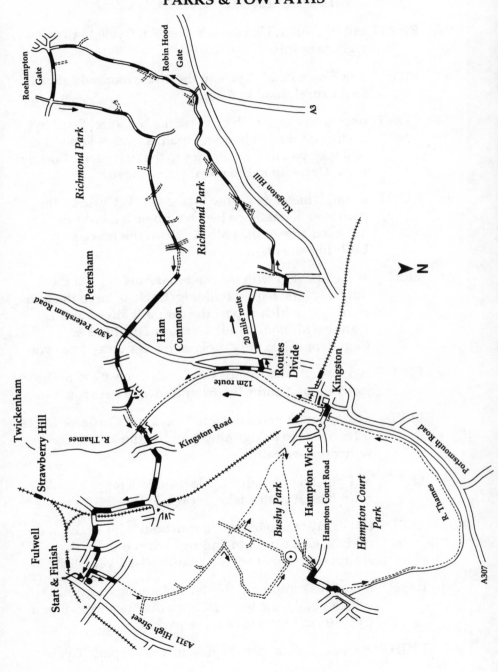

MIDDLESEX - 12 MILE ROUTE

0·0 RIGHT out of Church Hall into Princes Rd. **Cycle to the first right turn into Kings Road.**

0·1 RIGHT into Kings Road. **Cycle to the 2nd crossroads ahead and Laurel Road in 0·2m.**

0·3 CONT over crossroads with busy road into Laurel Road by cycling on the left hand footpath ahead of you which will take you to the entrance to the first park - Bushey Park. **Cycle up to the metal gates ahead.**

0·4 CONT through metal gates into Bushey Park. Cycle on the path ahead, passing a bench with no back, on the left hand side of the path. **Cycle to the fenced building ahead.**

0·6 LEFT at the junction with the road that runs around the outside of the fenced building. **Cycle 0·7m to the 2nd right turn which is past the car park ahead and is signposted 'Woodlands Gardens Disabled & Registered Cars only'** -this sign faces **away** from you.

1·3 RIGHT signposted 'Woodlands Gardens'. **Cycle 0·6m to the junction of 2 paths by the entrance to gardens.**

1·9 LEFT at junction of paths outside Woodland Gardens. **Cycle 0·2m over the bridge ahead and to the T junction with another path.**

2·1 LEFT at T junction of paths. **Cycle 0·4m to a large roundabout with a lake in themiddle.**

2·5 LEFT (1st exit) at the one way roundabout with a lake in the middle. **Cycle 0·5m to 2nd right turn onto path signposted 'No entry for unauthorised vehicles'.**

3·0 RIGHT onto path signposted 'No entry for unauthorised vehicles', take the left fork immediately ahead of you. **Cycle 0·7m to a gate into the park.**

3·7 RIGHT in front of metal gate to park to a stony path. **Cycle**

1·1m to a path on your left by a stream just after a children's play area.

4·8   LEFT   onto unsignposted path by a stream which leads to the gates to the park. **Cycle up to the gates.**

4·9   CONT   through gates to park and cross over the busy road ahead by using the pedestrian crossing on your left.

5·0   RIGHT   in front of huge gate to Hampton Court. **Cycle 0·4m on the road or pavement past Kings Arms PH on your left to a left turn onto the road running alongside the River Thames, just before a large road bridge over the river. This is our second park.**

5·4   LEFT   onto road running alongside the River Thames just before bridge over the river. **Cycle 2·6m on this path by the Thames to Kingston Bridge.**

8·0   RIGHT   at T junction taking the road onto Kingston Bridge you **MUST use the pedestrian crossing to cross this road. Cycle 0·3m or walk on the pavement to the 2nd left turn by Two Brewers PH.**

8·3   LEFT   by Two Brewers PH into road signposted 'No Through Road'. **Cycle to end via a small cycle lane.**

8·4   CONT   at T junction with one-way road by walking your bike down a very short one-way road ahead with the Outrigger PH on the left. **Cycle to a right turn at the bottom of this road.**

8·4   RIGHT   at road alongside the river, signposted 'No through road except cycles'. **Cycle 0·4m along this road & the bike path ahead to the T junction end just past Kingston Rowing Club.**

8·8   LEFT   at T junction with small road signposted Ham just past Kingston Rowing Club. **Cycle 0·4m to path along side the river by red post box & bench around tree.**

The 20m route turns right here - you turn left.

9·2   LEFT   onto the footpath running closest to the River Thames. **Cycle 0·8m along this path to the first footbridge over the River.**

10·0   LEFT   and up & onto the footbridge with special gulley to wheel your bike in - be careful going down the other side. **Walk over the bridge and cycle up to the traffic lights on the other side of the river.**

The 20m route re joins you here.

10·4   CONT   over traffic lights into Ferry Road. **Cycle 0·5m up Teddington High Street to a mini roundabout and into Waldergrave Road.**

10·9   RIGHT   at mini roundabout into Waldergrave Road. **Cycle 0·4m to 2nd left turn into Shackelgate Lane.**

11·3   LEFT   into Shackelgate Lane. **Cycle 0·3m to crossroads.**

11·6   LEFT   at crossroads with Stanley Road. **Cycle to 1st right into Princes Road by the advertising hoarding to your left.**

11·7   RIGHT   into Princes Road just by the large advertising hoarding. **Cycle 0·3m to the Church Hall.**

12·0   arrive back at the church hall.

End of 12m route.

MIDDLESEX - 20 MILE ROUTE

0·0   RIGHT   out of Church Hall into Princes Rd. **Cycle to the first right turn into Kings Road.**

0·1   RIGHT   into Kings Road. **Cycle 0·2m to the 2nd crossroads ahead and Laurel Road.**

0·3   CONT   over crossroads with busy road into Laurel Road by cycling on the left hand footpath ahead of you which will take you to the entrance to the first park - Bushey Park. **Cycle up to the metal gates ahead.**

0·4   CONT   through metal gates into Bushey Park. Cycle on the path ahead of you passing a bench with no back, on the left hand side of this path. **Cycle 0·2m to the fenced building ahead of you.**

0·6   LEFT   at the junction with the road that runs around the outside of the fenced building. **Cycle 0·7m to the 2nd right turn which is past the car park ahead and is signposted 'Woodlands Gardens Disabled & Registred Cars only'** -This sign faces **away** from you.

1·3   RIGHT   signposted 'Woodlands Gardens Registered & Disabled cars only'. **Cycle 0·6m to the junction of 2 paths by the entrance to gardens.**

1·9   LEFT   at junction of paths outside Woodland Gardens. **Cycle 0·2m over the bridge ahead and to the T junction with another path.**

2·1   LEFT   at T junction of paths. **Cycle 0·4m to a large roundabout with a lake in the centre.**

2·5   LEFT   at the one-way roundabout with a lake in the centre. **Take the 1st exit left off the roundabout and then take the 2nd right path in 0·5m signposted 'No entry for unauthorised vehicles'.**

3·0   RIGHT   onto path signposted 'No entry for unauthorised vehicles'. **Take the left fork immediately ahead of you. Cycle 0·7m to gate into park.**

3·7 RIGHT in front of metal gate to park onto a stony path. **Cycle 1·1m to a path on your left by a stream just after a children's play area.**

4·8 LEFT onto unsignposted path by a stream which leads to the gates to the park. **Cycle up to the gates.**

4·9 CONT through gates to park and cross over the busy road ahead by using the pedestrian crossing on your left.

5·0 RIGHT in front of huge gate to Hampton Court. **Cycle 0·4m on the road or pavement past Kings Arms PH on your left and shop to a left turn onto the road running alongside the River Thames just before a large road bridge over the river. This is our second park.**

5·4 LEFT onto road running alongside the River Thames just before bridge over the river. **Cycle 2·6m on this path by the Thames, to Kingston Bridge.**

8·0 RIGHT at T junction taking the road onto Kingston Bridge you **MUST** use the pedestrian crossing to cross this road. **Cycle 0·3m or walk on the pavement to the 2nd left turn by Two Brewers PH.**

8·3 LEFT by Two Brewers PH into road signposted 'No Through Road'. **Cycle to end via a small cycle lane.**

8·4 CONT at T junction with one-way road. **Walk your bike down a very short one-way road ahead with the Outrigger PH on your left to a right turn signposted 'No through road except for cycles'.**

8·4 RIGHT at road alongside the river signposted 'No through road except cycles'. **Cycle 0·4m along this road & the bike path ahead to T junction end with a small road which is just past Kingston Rowing Club.**

8·8 RIGHT at T junction with small road just past Kingston Rowing Club. **Cycle to 1st left into Bank Road by red letter box on the corner.**

The 12m route turns left here.

8·9   LEFT   into Bank Road. **Cycle 0·1m to crossroads end.**

9·0   CONT   over busy road into Latchmere Road . **Cycle 0·6m through roundabout ahead to the T junction end of Latchmere Road.**

9·6   RIGHT   at T junction. **Cycle 0·3m to mini roundabout with Kings Road.**

9·9   LEFT   at mini roundabout signposted Richmond Park & Kings Road. **Cycle 0·2m to T junction end.**

10·1   LEFT   and into our third park - Richmond Park. **Cycle to mini roundabout.**

10·2   RIGHT   at mini roundabout signposted Roehampton Gate. **Cycle 1·7m to mini roundabout.**

11·9   CONT   over roundabout signposted Roehampton Gate. **Cycle 1.2m to another mini roundabout.** Just before the roundabout ahead there is a cafe set back on the right hand side.

13·1   LEFT   at roundabout signposted Richmond gate. **Cycle 0·4m to 1st left at the next mini roundabout.**

13·5   LEFT   at mini roundabout signposted 'No admittance to unauthorised vehicles'. **Cycle 1m to right hand turn just past a large car park signposted Ham Gate.**

14·5   RIGHT   down road signposted Ham Gate. **Cycle 0·9m to a crossroads at the end of this road.**

15·3   CONT   over crossroads down hill signposted Ham Gate. **Cycle 0·9m through gates to Richmond Park into Ham Gate Avenue to traffic lights.**

16·2   CONT   at crossroads & traffic lights into Lock Road. **Cycle 0·6m to T junction end.**

16·8   LEFT   at T junction. **Cycle 0·1m to Dukes Avenue at crossroads end.**

16·9 RIGHT at crossroads into Dukes Avenue. **Cycle 1·1m to bike path (3rd left) signposted Teddington (cyclists only) & Teddington Lock.**

18·0 LEFT onto bike path signposted Teddington & Teddington Lock. **Cycle over bridge - use special gully for your bike, up to traffic lights.**

The 12m route rejoins you here.

18·4 CONT over traffic lights into Ferry Road. **Cycle 0·5m up Teddington High Street to a mini roundabout and into Waldergrave Road.**

18·9 RIGHT at mini roundabout into Waldergrave Road. **Cycle 0·4m to Shackelgate Lane which is 2nd left.**

19·3 LEFT into Shackelgate Lane. **Cycle 0·3m crossroads end.**

19·6 LEFT at crossroads with Stanley Road. **Cycle to 1st right into Princes Road by the advertising hoarding you can see to your left.**

19·7 RIGHT into Princes Road just by the large advertising hoarding. **Cycle to end and the Church Hall.**

20·0 arrive back at the Church Hall.

End of 20m route.

BANBURY TO THE RIVER WINDRUSH

A choice of routes through the delightful countryside south of Banbury. The rides consist of three loops so it is simple to add detours and extend or shorten the distance. Although the starting point is at Banbury, it can just as easily be approached from Witney, west of Oxford, at the southern extent of the long route.

The 20m route takes in a straightforward circuit to Barford St. Michael and back to Banbury via Bloxham. The 42m ride continues south through Chipping Norton then due east to Middle Barton before heading north to Banbury. The longer route crosses the River Evenlode and reaches Witney and the River Windrush at roughly the half way stage. It then passes to the west of Woodstock and Blenheim Palace to rejoin the 42m route at Midle Barton.

There are no major hills although parts are undulating. The whole route is on minor roads and country lanes with plenty of pleasant villages along the way.

Map	OS LR 164 Oxford, 151 Stratford.
Distance	20, 42 or 63 miles.
Start/Finish	Town Hall, High Street, Banbury.

Railway Access

Banbury - from Birmingham to the north and London Marylebone.

Ascott-under-Wynchwood - on the west of the long route, trains on the Worcester line from Oxford.

Places to see

Banbury. Think of Cakes and Crosses. A busy agricultural centre with some fine buildings and a Village Museum in the Courthouse.

Broughton Castle. A moated 14th century manor house.

Bloxham. A pleasant village with rows of thatched stone cottages on narrow lanes.

Chipping Norton. The highest town in Oxfordshire. see the Almshouses on the lane leading to St. Mary's Church.

Great Tew. A classic English village of thatched cottages and beautiful gardens. In the centre of the 42m route loop.

Minster Lovell Hall. A 15th century ruin in a idyllic location on the banks of the River Windrush.

Roman Villa, North Leigh. Renowned mosaic floor decorations.

Blenheim Palace, Woodstock. 1.5m off the long route. The largest house in the Country, built for the Duke of Marlborough with magnificent grounds by Capability Brown.

Tourist Information Office, Banbury Museum, Banbury 0295 259855.

Refreshments

Pubs & Cafes, Banbury.

Pubs, Wigginton, Barford St. Michael, Bloxham - 20m route.

Pubs & shops, Chipping Norton - 17m.

Pubs & shops, Witney - 35m, long route.

Pub, Middle Barton - 29m, 42m route. 50m, 63m route.

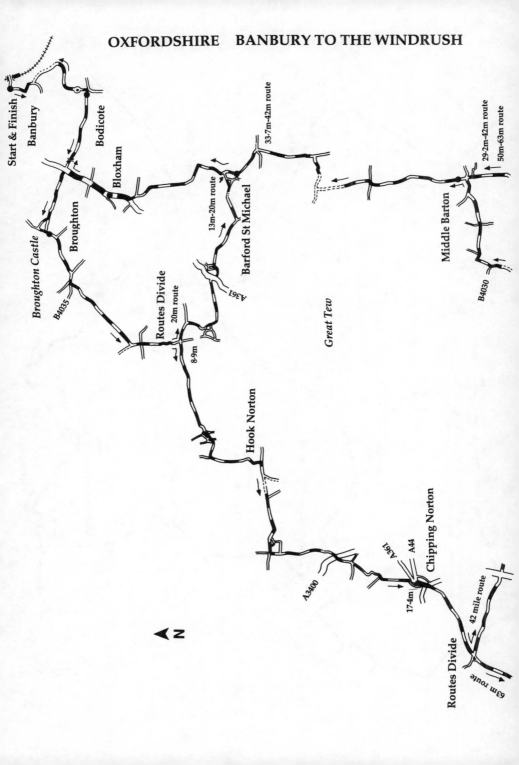

OXFORDSHIRE   BANBURY TO THE WINDRUSH

OXFORDSHIRE   BANBURY TO THE WINDRUSH

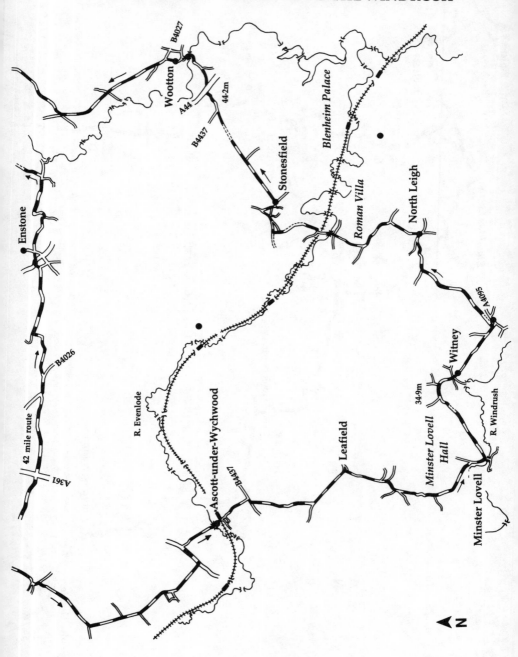

Enstone

B4026

42 mile route

A361

Wootton

B4027

A44

4·2m

B4437

Stonesfield

Blenheim Palace

Roman Villa

North Leigh

A4095

Witney

R. Windrush

3·9m

Minster Lovell Hall

Minster Lovell

Leafield

R. Evenlode

Ascott-under-Wychwood

B4437

N

OXFORDSHIRE - 20 MILE ROUTE

0·1   RIGHT   at traffic lights signposted Adderbury A4260.
Cycle 0·2m to garage and set of traffic lights.

0·3   LEFT   at garage and lights signposted Tramway Industrial
Estate. **Cycle 0·2m to left turn into Bankside.**

0·5   LEFT   into Bankside. **Cycle 1·3m to roundabout.**

1·8   CONT   across roundabout signposted Bodicote ½.
Cycle 0·2m to right turn signposted Broughton.

2·0   RIGHT   signposted Broughton. **Cycle 1·4m to crossroads
with A361.**

3·4   CONT   over crossroads with A361 onto unsignposted road.
**Cycle 1·1m into Broughton & one way system in
village leading to T junction end.**

4·5   LEFT   at T junction signposted Tadmarton 3. **Cycle 1·8m
to third left turn for Tadmarton Heath 1 ½.**

6·3   LEFT   signposted Tadmarton Heath 1 ½ . **Cycle 1·8m to
crossroads end.**

8·1   CONT   over crossroads signposted Wigginton 1 ¼.
Cycle 0·8m to crossroads end. *Caution descent
ahead.*

8·9   LEFT   at crossroads signpostedMilcombe 1 ½. **Cycle 0·4m
to first unsignposted right turn.**

The longer routes turn right here - you turn left.

9·3   RIGHT   Signposted Unsuitable for Heavy Motor Vehicles.
Cycle 0·3m to unsignposted T junction end.

9·6   LEFT   at unsignposted T junction opposite The Old Rectory.
Cycle 1·1m to unsignposted T junction end.

10·7   RIGHT   at unsignposted T junction with A361. **Cycle 0·1m
to left turn signposted The Barfords.**

10·8   LEFT   signposted The Barfords. **Cycle 1·2m to left turn signposted Barfords 1.**

12·0   LEFT   signposted Barfords 1. **Cycle 1m to T junction.**

13·0   LEFT   at unsignposted T junction . **Cycle 1·9m to T junction end with A361.**

14·9   RIGHT at T junction onto A361 signposted Banbury. **Cycle 1·8m to right turn signposted Bodicote.**

16·7   RIGHT signposted Bodicote. **Cycle 1·5m to T junction.**

18·2   LEFT   at T junction signposted Banbury 4. **Cycle 0·2m to roundabout end.**

18.4   CONT   across roundabout. **Cycle 1·3m to T junction.**

19·7   RIGHT at T junction into Swan Road. **Cycle 0·2m to right turn at traffic lights.**

19·9   RIGHT at traffic lights & into Upper Windsor Street. **Cycle 0·2m to left turn at 2nd set of lights.**

20·1   LEFT   at traffic lights into Banbury High Street. **Cycle 0·1m to Town Hall.**

End of 20m route.

OXFORDSHIRE - 42 MILE ROUTE

0·0   CONT   to traffic lights at bottom of High Street.

0·1   RIGHT   at traffic lights signposted Adderbury A4260. **Cycle 0·2m to garage and 2nd set of traffic lights.**

0·3   LEFT   at garage and lights signposted Tramway Industrial Estate. **Cycle 0·2m to left turn into Bankside.**

0·5   LEFT   into Bankside. **Cycle 1·3m to roundabout.**

1·8   CONT   across roundabout signposted Bodicote ½. **Cycle 0·2m to right turn signposted Broughton.**

2·0   RIGHT   signposted Broughton. **Cycle 1·4m to crossroads end with A361.**

3·4   CONT   over crossroads with A361 onto unsignposted road. **Cycle 1·1m into Broughton & one way system leading to T junction end.**

4·5   LEFT   at T junction signposted Tadmarton 3. **Cycle 1·8m to third left turn for Tadmarton Heath 1 ½.**

6·3   LEFT   signposted Tadmarton Heath 1 ½ . **Cycle 1·8m to crossroads end.**

8·1   CONT   over crossroads signposted Wigginton 1 ¼. **Cycle 0·8m to crossroads end.** *Caution descent ahead.*

8·9   RIGHT   at crossroads signposted Hook Norton 2. **Cycle 5·3m through Hook Norton village to left turn signposted Over Norton 2 & Chipping Norton 3.**

The 22m route turns left here - you turn right.

14·2   LEFT   signposted Over Norton 2 & Chipping Norton 3. **Cycle 1·3m to staggered crossroads with A3400.**

15·5   CONT   over A3400 & staggered crossroads signposted Over Norton 1. **Cycle 1·6m to roundabout end.**

17·1   RIGHT   at roundabout (3rd exit) signposted A44 Evesham. **Cycle 0·3m to left turn signposted Burford A361.**

17·4   LEFT   signposted Burford A361 by Ladies Toilets.
Cycle 0·1m to right turn at mini roundabout.

17·5   RIGHT at mini roundabout signposted Stow 10 (B4450).
Cycle 1·6m to left turn signposted Lidstone.

19·1   LEFT   signposted Lidstone. **Cycle 1·5m to crossroads.**

The 63m route continues here - you turn left.

20·6   CONT   over crossroads signposted Lidstone 3. **Cycle 1·6m
to T junction end with B4026.**

22·2   RIGHT at unsignposted T junction with B4026. **Cycle 0·3m
to first left signposted Enstone 3.**

22·5   LEFT   signposted Enstone 3. **Cycle 2m to T junction.**

24·5   LEFT   at unsignposted T junction. **Cycle 0·1m to
T junction end with A44.**

24·6   RIGHT at T junction signposted Woodstock 7. **Cycle 0·2m
to left turn signposted Cleveley 1.**

24·8   LEFT   signposted Cleveley 1. **Cycle 0·1m to crossroads.**

24·9   CONT   over crossroads signposted Cleveley ½. **Cycle 0·7m
to left turn signposted Radford 1 ¼.**

25.6   LEFT   signposted Radford 1 ¼. **Cycle 1m to crossroads.**

26·6   LEFT   at crossroads signposted Gagingwell ¾. **Cycle 0·8m
to T junction end with B4030.**

27.4   RIGHT at T junction onto B4030. **Cycle 1·8m to left turn
inMiddle Barton signposted Worton.**

29·2   LEFT   into Worton Road signposted Worton. **Cycle 1·8m
to staggered crossroads end.**

30·0   CONT   over staggered crossroads signposted Over Worton.
Cycle 1·1m to small grass triangle.

Caution! - closed gates on descent ahead.

32·1 RIGHT at unsignposted T junction at bottom of hill. **Cycle 0·6m to T junction with Oxfordshire Cycleway.**

32·7 LEFT at T junction signposted Oxfordshire Cycleway. **Cycle 1·1m to staggered crossroads end with B4031.**

33·7 CONT over staggered crossroads with B4031 signposted Barfords. **Cycle 3m to T junction end with A361.**

36·9 RIGHT at T junction onto A361 signposted Banbury 4. **Cycle 1·8m to right turn signposted Bodicote.**

38·7 RIGHT signposted Bodicote. **Cycle 1·5m to T junction.**

40·2 LEFT at T junction signposted Banbury. **Cycle 0·2m to roundabout end.**

40.4 CONT across roundabout. **Cycle 1·3m to T junction.**

41·7 RIGHT at T junction into Swan Road. **Cycle 0·2m to right turn at traffic lights.**

41·9 RIGHT at traffic lights & into Upper Windsor Street. **Cycle 0·2m to left turn at 2nd set of lights.**

42·1 LEFT at traffic lights into Banbury High Street. **Cycle 0·1m to Town Hall.**

End of 42m route.

OXFORDSHIRE - 63 MILE ROUTE

0·0   CONT   to traffic lights at bottom of High Street.

0·1   RIGHT   at traffic lights signposted A4260. **Cycle 0·2m to garage and 2nd set of traffic lights.**

0·3   LEFT   at garage and lights signposted Tramway Industrial Estate. **Cycle 0·2m to left turn into Bankside.**

0·5   LEFT   into Bankside. **Cycle 1·3m to roundabout.**

1·8   CONT   across roundabout signposted Bodicote ½. **Cycle 0·2m to first right turn signposted Broughton.**

2·0   RIGHT   signposted Broughton. **Cycle 1·4m to crossroads end with A361.**

3·4   CONT   over crossroads with A361 onto unsignposted road. **Cycle 1·1m into Broughton & one way system in village leading to T junction end.**

4·5   LEFT   at T junction signposted Tadmarton 3. **Cycle 1·8m to third left turn signposted Tadmarton Heath 1 ½.**

6·3   LEFT   signposted Tadmarton Heath 1 ½ . **Cycle 1·8m to crossroads end.**

8·1   CONT   over crossroads signposted Wigginton 1 ¼. **Cycle 0·8m to crossroads end.** *Caution descent ahead.*

8·9   RIGHT   crossroads signposted Hook Norton 2. **Cycle 5·3m through Hook Norton village to left turn signposted Over Norton 2 & Chipping Norton 3.**

The 22m route turns left here - you turn right.

14·2   LEFT   signposted Over Norton 2 & Chipping Norton 3. **Cycle 1·3m to staggered crossroads end with A3400.**

15·5   CONT   over A3400 & staggered crossroads signposted Over Norton 1. **Cycle 1·6m to roundabout end.**

17·1   RIGHT   at roundabout, 3rd exit, signposted A44 Evesham.

Cycle 0·3m to left turn signposted Burford A361.

17·4 LEFT signposted Burford A361 by Ladies Toilets. **Cycle 0·1m to right turn at mini roundabout.**

17·5 RIGHT at mini roundabout, 2nd exit, signposted Stow 10. **Cycle 4·1m to left turn signposted Lyneham 1 ½.**

19·1 *The 42m route turns left here - you continue.*

21·6 LEFT signposted Lyneham 1 ½. **Cycle 2·3m to T junction end with A361.**

23·9 LEFT at T junction & onto A361. **Cycle 0·5m to first right signposted Ascott-under-Wychwood.**

24·4 RIGHT signposted Ascott-under-Wychwood. **Cycle 1·5m to T junction end.**

25·9 RIGHT at T junction signposted Leafield. **Cycle 0·1m to left turn signposted Leafield.**

26·0 LEFT signposted Leafield. **Cycle 1·2m to T junction end.**

27·2 LEFT at T junction signposted Leafield 1. **Cycle 0·8m to T junction end.**

28·0 RIGHT at T junction signposted Fordwells 1. **Cycle 0·8m to right turn signposted Fordwells ¼.**

28·8 RIGHT signposted Fordwells ¼. **Cycle 0·2m to T junction.**

29·0 LEFT signposted Asthall Leigh ¾. **Cycle 0·8m to left turn signpostedMinster Lovell.**

29·8 LEFT by converted church signpostedMinster Lovell. **Cycle 1·0m to T junction end.**

30·8 RIGHT at unsignposted T junction. **Cycle 0·3m to unsignposted 1st left turn.**

31·1 LEFT unsignposted past Swan PH. **Cycle 1·5m to T junction end.**

32·6 RIGHT at T junction signposted Crawley. **Cycle 0·5m to**

staggered crossroads end by Lamb PH.

33·1 CONT over staggered crossroads signposted Oxfordshire Cycleway. **Cycle 1·4m to roundabout end.**

34·5 CONT at roundabout 2nd exit signposted Oxford 13. **Cycle 0·3m to left turn at double mini roundabout.**

34·8 LEFT at double roundabout signposted A4095 Bicester. **Cycle 0·1m to 1st left turn signposted New Yatt.**

34·9 LEFT signposted New Yatt. **Cycle 2·7m to left turn just after Woodman PH in North Leigh village.**

37·6 LEFT into Church Road. **Cycle 0·6m to T junction end.**

38·2 LEFT at T junction signposted Wilcote 1 ¼. **Cycle 2·7m to T junction end signposted Stonesfield ½.**

40·9 RIGHT at T junction signposted Stonesfield ½. **Cycle 0·5m to right turn signposted Combe 1 ¾ by Avia garage.**

41·4 RIGHT signposted Combe 1 ¾ by Avia garage. **Cycle 20 metres to T junction end.**

41·4 RIGHT at T junction unsignposted. **Cycle 0·3m to War Memorial.**

41·7 CONT at War Memorial signposted Woodstock 4 ½. **Cycle 2·2m to T junction end with B4437.**

43·9 RIGHT at T junction onto B4437. **Cycle 0·3m to staggered crossroads end with A44.**

44·2 CONT over staggered crossroads signposted Wootton. **Cycle 1·4m to T junction end signposted Glympton 1.**

45·6 LEFT at T junction signposted Glympton 1. **Cycle 0·2m to 1st right turn signposted Barton 4.**

45·8 RIGHT signposted Barton 4 into Tew Lane. **Cycle 1·8m to right turn signposted Barton 2.**

48·0 RIGHT signposted Bartons 2. **Cycle 2m to crossroads end in Middle Barton.**

50·0 CONT over crossroads with B4030 signposted Warton.
Cycle 1·8m to staggered crossroads end.

51·8 CONT over staggered crossroads signposted Over Worton.
Cycle 1·1m to small grass triangle.

Caution! - closed gates on descent ahead.

52·9 RIGHT at unsignposted T junction with grass triangle. **Cycle
0·6m to T junction with Oxfordshire cycleway.**

53·5 LEFT at T junction signposted Oxfordshire Cycleway.
Cycle 1·1m to staggered crossroads end with B4031.

54·7 CONT over staggered crossroads with B4031 signposted
Barfords. **Cycle 3m to T junction end with A361.**

57·7 RIGHT at T junction onto A361 signposted Banbury 4.
Cycle 1·8m to right turn signposted Bodicote.

59·5 RIGHT signposted Bodicote. **Cycle 1·5m to T junction.**

61·0 LEFT at T junction signposted Banbury. **Cycle 0·2m to
roundabout end.**

61·2 CONT across roundabout. **Cycle 1·3m to T junction.**

62·5 RIGHT at T junction into Swan Close Road. **Cycle 0·2m to
right turn at traffic lights.**

62·7 RIGHT at traffic lights & into Upper Windsor Street.
Cycle 0·2m to left turn at 2nd set of lights .

62·9 LEFT at traffic lights into Banbury High Street.
Cycle 0·1m to Town Hall.

End of 63m route.

MARK MOOR TO FROME VIA CHEDDAR GORGE & RETURN VIA GLASTONBURY

This ride starts and finishes at Highbridge, close to Burnham-on-Sea, a haven for camping and caravanning. The routes follow direct and straight roads and is therefore quite fast, with a few hills and glorious views.

You start on the moors east of Highbridge, over the River Axe valley, and climb the Mendips at Cheddar Gorge. From here the ride follows a good and straight B road north of the Cathedral City of Wells. At Shepton Mallet the 58m route heads south to Evercreech for the return leg. The longer route continues east to cover the 26m stretch to Frome. At Frome, the 86m route turns south for 8m to go through Bruton and over a hilly section before rejoining the shorther route at Evercreech.

Cross the Fosse Way and over Kennard Moor to enjoy views of Glastonbury Tor on the approach to the town. From Glastonbury it is an easy 13m across the Somerset Levels back to Highbridge.

Map	OS LR 183 Yeovil & Frome.
	OS LR 182 Weston-Super-Mare & Bridgwater.
Distance	58 or 86 miles.
Start/Finish	Highbridge Community Centre, Market Street, Highbridge.

Railway Access

Highbridge - trains from Bristol to the north and Exeter to the south.

Frome & Bruton - trains from London Paddington via Reading & Newbury.

Places to see

Burnham-on-Sea. All the trappings of a seaside resort.

Cheddar Gorge, Cheddar. Home of the famous cheese, at the foot of the spectacular Gorge in the Mendip hills. Showcaves, views and tourists galore.

Wells. A 3m diversion from the main route but well worth a detour to see England's smallest city and its magnificent 12th century cathedral.

Wookey Hole. 1m outside of Wells and famous for its limestone caves.

Glastonbury. A magical place where the mystical and ancient atmosphere is genuinely tangible. *Glastonbury Abbey* is the first Christian Sanctuary in the British Isles with a history steeped in legend. *The Tor* is over 500 feet above sea level and provides panoramic views over glastonbury and the moors.

The Mendips & Somerset Levels. Features which add a natural splendour to this glorious ride.

Tourist Information Office, South Esplanade, Burnham-on-Sea 0278 787852. The Tribunal, Glastonbury 0458 832954.

Refreshment

Tea Shops, Cheddar Gorge - 12.3m.

Poachers Pocket PH, where routes divide - 29.5m.

Pubs, shops & cafes, Frome - 37.1m, long route.

Blue Ball PH, Bruton - 52.6m, long route.

Pubs, shops & cafes, Glastonbury - 46m, 58m route. 71m, 86m route.

Coopers Arms PH, Highbridge - opposite start & finish.

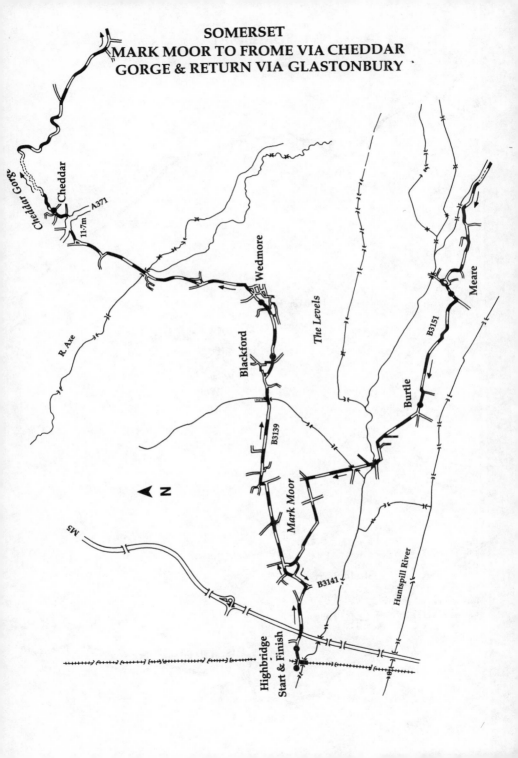

SOMERSET
MARK MOOR TO FROME VIA CHEDDAR
GORGE & RETURN VIA GLASTONBURY

SOMERSET

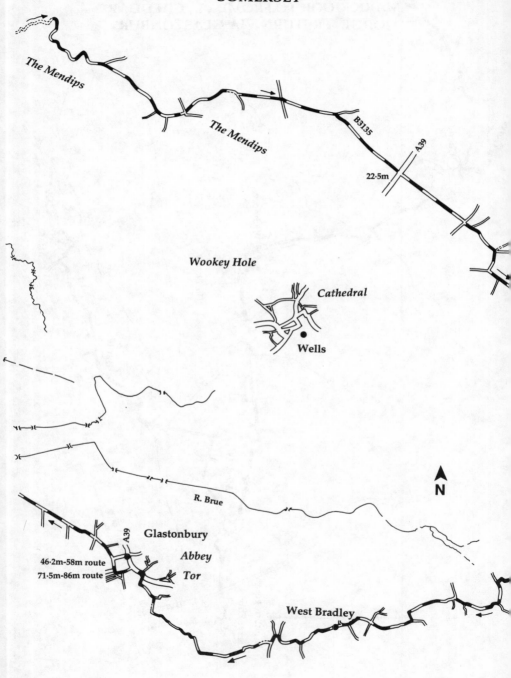

The Mendips

The Mendips

B3135

A39

22·5m

Wookey Hole

Cathedral

Wells

N

R. Brue

Glastonbury

A39

Abbey

Tor

46·2m-58m route
71·5m-86m route

West Bradley

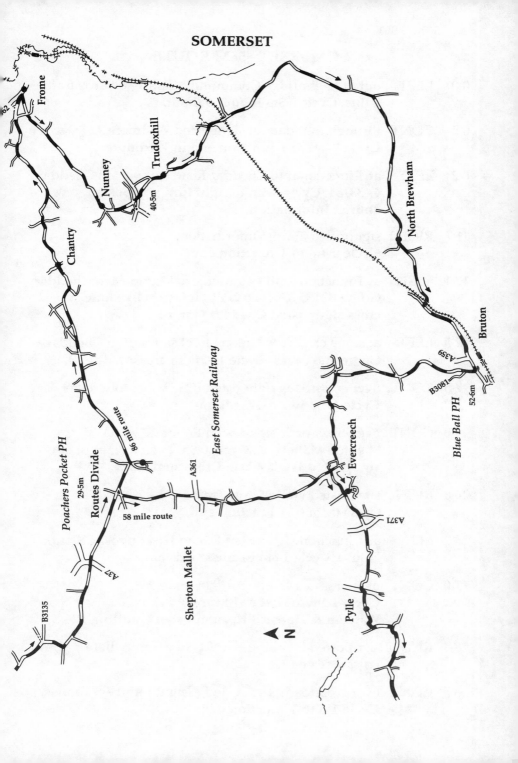

SOMERSET

Frome

Trudoxhill

Nunney

40·5m

Chantry

North Brewham

Bruton

A359

B3081

52·6m

Blue Ball PH

Poachers Pocket PH

29·5m

86 mile route

Routes Divide

58 mile route

A361

East Somerset Railway

Evercreech

A371

Shepton Mallet

A37

B3135

N

Pylle

SOMERSET - 58M ROUTE

0·0 LEFT out of Highbridge Community Centre towards traffic lights. **Cycle 0·5m to roundabout.**

0·5 CONT through roundabout signposted Wedmore 7 ½. **Cycle 7·7m to T junction end in Wedmore.**

8·2 LEFT at T junction into Cheddar Road signposted Cheddar 4. B3151. **Cycle 3·5m to right turn signposted Tourist Information.**

11·7 RIGHT signposted Tourist Information. **Cycle 0·4m to T junction end.**

12·1 RIGHT at T junction with War Memorial signposted Cheddar Gorge B3135. **Cycle 0·2m to left turn by stone cross signposted Cheddar Gorge.**

12·3 LEFT at stone cross into Union Street signposted Cheddar Gorge and caves. **Cycle 10·2m to crossroads end.**

22·5 CONT over crossroads signposted B3135 Shepton Mallet 6. **Cycle 1·5m to crossroads end.**

24·0 CONT over crossroads signposted Frome 12 ½, B3135 & Shepton Mallet 4 ½. **Cycle 0·8m to first right turn signposted Wells 4 ½ & Crosscombe 2 ¾.**

24·8 RIGHT signposted Wells 4 ½ & Crosscombe 2 ¾. **Cycle 0·4m to T junction end.**

25.2 LEFT at T junction signposted Frome 11 ¼ opposite Station House. **Cycle 1·8m to crossroads end.**

27·0 CONT over crossroads signposted Frome 9 ½. **Cycle 1·4m to first right turn, by the Waggon & Horses PH, signposted Doulting 1 ½.**

28·4 RIGHT signposted Doulting 1 ½. **Cycle to immediate crossroads end.**

28·5 CONT over crossroads signposted Weight Limit 7·5 Tonnes. **Cycle 1m to T junction end.**

29·5 RIGHT at unsignposted T junction by Poachers Pocket PH.
Cycle 0·5m to T junction end.

30·0 RIGHT at T junction signposted A361. **Cycle 0·1m to
immediate unsignposted left turn by Abbey Barn
Inn.**

30·1 LEFT at unsignposted left turn. **Cycle 2·7m to second
right signposted Evercreech ½.**

32·8 RIGHT at turn signposted Evercreech ½. **Cycle 0·6m
to staggered crossroads end.**

33·4 CONT over staggered crossroads into Leighton Lane (just to
your right). **Cycle to crossroads end.**

34·6 CONT over crossroads signposted Pylle 1 ¼. **Cycle 1·3m
to T junction.**

35·9 LEFT onto busy unsignposted road. **Cycle 0·1m to first
right signposted Pylle Manor.**

36·0 RIGHT signposted Pylle Manor. **Cycle 0·7m to T junction.**

36·7 LEFT at T junction signposted East Pennard 1 ½.
Cycle 0·4m to T junction end.

37·1 RIGHT at T junction signposted East Pennard ¾. **Cycle 0·9m
to left turn signposted Glastonbury 7 ¼.**

38·0 LEFT signposted Glastonbury 7 ¼.
Cycle 1·1m to T junction end.

39·1 RIGHT at T junction signposted Glastonbury 6 ¼. **Cycle 2·7m
to left turn signposted Glastonbury 3 ¼.**

41·8 LEFT at turn signposted Glastonbury 3 ¼.
Cycle 0·1m to T junction end.

41·9 LEFT at T junction signposted Baltonsborough 1 ¼.
Cycle 0·2m to first right by red Post Box.

42·0 RIGHT onto unsignposted road by Post Box.
Cycle 2·7m to T junction.

44·7 LEFT at unsignposted T junction opposite Glastonbury Tor. **Cycle 0·6m to T junction end.**

45·3 LEFT at unsignposted T junction. **Cycle 0·3m to mini roundabout.**

45·6 LEFT at mini roundabout signposted Town Centre. **Cycle 0·4m to mini roundabout.**

46·0 RIGHT at mini roundabout signposted Town Centre. **Cycle 0·2m to mini roundabout opposite Crown Hotel.**

46·2 LEFT at mini roundabout signposted Toilets & Public Library. **Cycle 4·7m to left turn signposted Burtle.**

50·9 LEFT signposted Burtle 2 ½. **Cycle 0·2m to T junction.**

51·1 LEFT at unsignposted T junction opposite wooden farm entrance. **Cycle 0·3m to first right signposted Burtle 2.**

51·4 RIGHT signposted Burtle 2. **Cycle 2·9m to T junction.**

54·3 LEFT at T junction signposted Highbridge. **Cycle 0·4m to crossroads end.**

54·7 CONT over crossroads signposted Highbridge 3 ½. **Cycle 1·3m to left turn signposted Highbridge 2 ½.**

56·0 LEFT at turn signposted Highbridge 2 ½. **Cycle 0·4m to T junction end.**

56·4 LEFT at T junction signposted Highbridge 2 ¼ by Watchfield PH. **Cycle 1·5m to roundabout .**

57·9 CONT over roundabout signposted Highbridge B3139. **Cycle 0·4m to left turn into hall in Highbridge.**

58·3 LEFT into Highbridge Community Centre.

End of 58m route.

SOMERSET - 86M ROUTE

0·0   LEFT   out of Highbridge Community Centre towards traffic lights. **Cycle 0·5m to roundabout.**

0·5   CONT   over roundabout signposted Wedmore 7 ½. **Cycle 7·7m to T junction end in Wedmore.**

8·2   LEFT   at T junction into Cheddar Road signposted Cheddar 4. **Cycle 3·5m to a right turn signposted Tourist Information.**

11·7   RIGHT   signposted Tourist Information. **Cycle 0·4m to T junction end.**

12·1   RIGHT   at T junction with War Memorial signposted Cheddar Gorge. **Cycle 0·2m to left turn signposted Cheddar Gorge.**

12·3   LEFT   at stone cross into Union Street signposted Cheddar Gorge and caves. **Cycle 10·2m to crossroads end.**

22·5   CONT   over crossroads signposted B3135 SheptonMallet 6. **Cycle 1·5m to crossroads end.**

24·0   CONT   over crossroads signposted Frome 12 ½ (B3135) and SheptonMallet 4 ½. **Cycle 0·8m to first right turn signposted Wells 4 ½, Crosscombe 2 ¾.**

24·8   RIGHT   signposted Wells 4 ½, Crosscombe 2 ¾. **Cycle 0·4m to T junction end.**   ˙

25·2   LEFT   at T junction signposted Frome 11 ¼ opposite Station House. **Cycle 1·8m to crossroads end.**

27·0   CONT   over crossroads signposted Frome 9 ½. **Cycle 2m to staggered crossroads end.**

The 58m route turns off at first right after crossroads, you continue.

29·0   CONT   over staggered crossroads signposted Frome 8. **Cycle 5·3m to crossroads end.**

34·3 CONT over crossroads signposted Frome 2 ¾.
Cycle 2·7m to mini roundabout end.

37·0 RIGHT at mini roundabout signposted all other routes.
Cycle 0·1m to right turn after traffic lights.

Cycle into Frome from here.

37·1 RIGHT into Nunney Road signposted Nunney 2 ¾. **Cycle 3·4m to left turn in front of Theobold Arms PH.**

40·5 LEFT down road signposted dead end and subway/cycles. **Cycle under A361 via subway through gate to immediate T junction.**

40·7 LEFT at unsignposted T junction. **Cycle 5·4m through Trudoxhill to T junction end.**

46·1 RIGHT at T junction signposted Brution.
Cycle 6·3m to T junction end.

52·4 LEFT at T junction with A359 signposted Brution ¼.
Cycle 0·2m to right turn opposite Blue Ball PH.

52·6 RIGHT into Coombe Street, opposite Blue Ball PH, before one way system. **Cycle 0·2m to first right turn.**

Cycle into Brution from here.

52·8 RIGHT at unsignposted right turn by Overdale House.
Cycle 3·3m to T junction end.

55·5 LEFT at T junction signposted Westcombe ½ & Evercreech 2 ¼. **Cycle 1·9m to T junction end.**

57·4 RIGHT at T junction signposted Doulting 2 ¾. **Cycle 0·2m to first left turn signposted Evercreech ½.**

The 58m route rejoins here.

57·6 LEFT at turn signposted Evercreech ½.
Cycle 0·5m to staggered crossroads end.

58·1 CONT over staggered crossroads into Leighton Lane (just to the right). **Cycle 0·4m to left turn signposted Leighton lane.**

58·5 LEFT at turn by corner shop (after Circle K). **Cycle 0·8m to crossroads end.**

59·7 CONT over crossroads signposted Pylle 1 ¼. **Cycle 1·3m to T junction end.**

61·0 LEFT onto busy unsignposted road. **Cycle 0·1m to first right signposted Pylle Manor.**

61·1 RIGHT signposted Pylle Manor. **Cycle 0·7m to T junction.**

61·8 LEFT at T junction signposted East Pennard 1 ½. **Cycle 0·4m to T junction.**

62·2 RIGHT at T junction signposted East Pennard ¾. **Cycle 0·9m to left turn signposted Glastonbury 7 ¼.**

63·1 LEFT signposted Glastonbury 7 ¼. **Cycle 1·1m to T junction end.**

64·2 RIGHT at T junction ignposted Glastonbury 6 ¼. **Cycle 2·7m to left turn signposted Glastonbury 3 ¼.**

66·9 LEFT signposted Glastonbury 3 ¼. **Cycle 0·1m to T junction end.**

67·0 LEFT at T junction signposted Baltonsborough 1 ¼. **Cycle 0·2m to first right by red Post Box.**

67·2 RIGHT onto unsignposted road by Post Box. **Cycle 2·7m to T junction end.**

69·9 LEFT at unsignposted T junction opposite Glastonbury Tor. **Cycle 0·6m to unsignposted T junction end.**

70·5 LEFT at unsignposted T junction. **Cycle 0·3m to mini roundabout.**

70·8 LEFT at mini roundabout signposted Town Centre. **Cycle 0·4m to mini roundabout.**

71·3 RIGHT at mini roundabout signposted Town Centre. **Cycle**

0·2m to mini roundabout opposite Crown Hotel.

71·5   LEFT   at mini roundabout signposted Toilets & Public Library. **Cycle 4·7m to left turn signposted Shapswick.**

76·3   LEFT   at turn signposted Burtle 2 ½. **Cycle 0·2m to T junction end.**

76·5   LEFT   at T junction opposite wooden farm entrance. **Cycle 0·3m to first right signposted Burtle 2.**

76·8   RIGHT   at turn signposted Burtle 2. **Cycle 2·9m to T junction.**

82·0   LEFT   at T junction signposted Highbridge. **Cycle 0·4m to crossroads end.**

82·4   CONT   over crossroads signposted Highbridge 3 ½. **Cycle 1·3m to left turn signposted Highbridge 2 ½.**

83·7   LEFT   at turn signposted Highbridge 2 ½. **Cycle 0·4m to T junction.**

84·1   LEFT   at T junction signposted Highbridge 2 ¼, by Watchfield PH. **Cycle 1·5m to roundabout.**

85·6   CONT   over roundabout signposted Highbridge B3139. **Cycle 0·4m to left turn into hall in Highbridge.**

86·1   LEFT   into Highbridge Community Centre.

End of 86m route.

SUFFOLK SKIES & CONSTABLE COUNTRY

This is an ideal weekend ride - stay at the Queens House bed & breakfast, literally yards from the start and finish point in Bures. All three rides offer rolling countryside, quiet lanes, picturesque villages and plenty of options for expanding or shortening the distance you would like to cover.

The 16m route is a straightforward circuit out to Boxford and Stoke-by-Nayland to return parallel to the River Stour and the Essex border. The longer routes head north from Boxford to the attractive town of Lavenham, known for its splendid timber-framed buildings, where four miles later the 38m route soon turns back at Preston St Mary.

The long route heads to the half way point at Stowmarket through the isolated lanes to the south-west of this Suffolk town. From here it is south by a windy and attractive route to Hadleigh and the River Brett. Single track country lanes take you south of Hadleigh to re-cross the river and enter Stoke-by-Nayland where the church was one of Constable's favourite subjects. From here we rejoin the shorter routes to return to Bures through Nayland, another pretty village with a cloth making heritage and interesting buildings.

Maps	OS LR155 Bury St Edmunds & Sudbury.
	OS LR168 Colchester & Blackwater.
Distance	16, 38 or 64 miles.
Start/Finish	Bures Village Hall, Nayland Road.

Railway Access

Bures - trains on Sudbury line from London Liverpool Street.

Stowmarket - northern extent of long route, trains from Cambridge to the west and Ipswich from the east.

Places to see

Lavenham. Flourished as a rich wool and cloth making centre from the 14th to 16th centuries. The wealth has long gone but the legacy of half-timbered Tudor and medieval buildings lives on. The Priory and the Guildhall are of particular note. It is also a tea-lovers paradise with no less than ten to choose from.

Museum of East Anglian Rural Life, Stowmarket. A 70 acre open air museum with a watermill, craft workshops and working exhibits to bring the past alive.

Wolves Wood, Hadleigh. 1.5m east off A1071 Ipswich Road. A RSPB reserve located in an ancient woodland coppice. The best time to visit is Spring - see the wild flowers, including orchids, and there are several nightingale territories.

Hadleigh. A town of Saxon origins with many fine buildings, including St.Mary's Church, the Guildhall and Deanery Tower. The High Street has examples of the East Anglian plaster craft called pargetting.

Tourist Information Office, Wilkes Way, Stowmarket 0449 676800. Toppesfield Hall, Hadleigh 0473 822922.

Refreshments

Tea shops & Angel PH, Lavenham - 14.2m, 16m & 38m routes.

Pubs & shops, Boxford - 21.2m, 16m & 38m routes.

Pubs, shops & cafes, Stowmarket - 30m, 64m route.

Pubs & shops, Hadleigh - 47m, 64m route.

Angel Hotel, Stoke-by-Nayland - 9m, 30m, 58m.

SUFFOLK
SUFFOLK SKIES & CONSTABLE COUNTRY

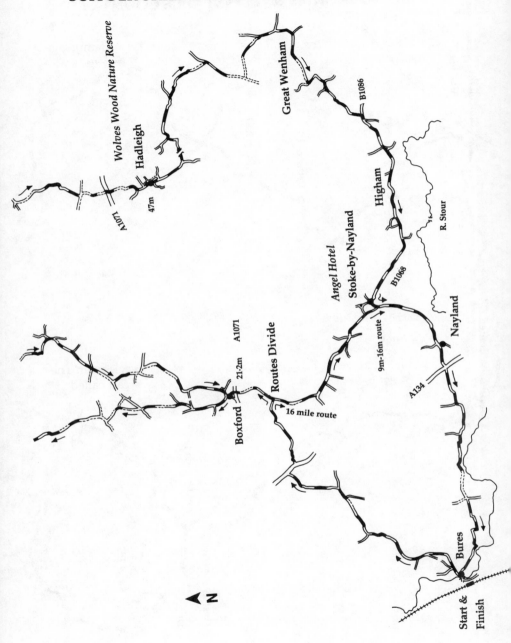

SUFFOLK
SUFFOLK SKIES & CONSTABLE COUNTRY

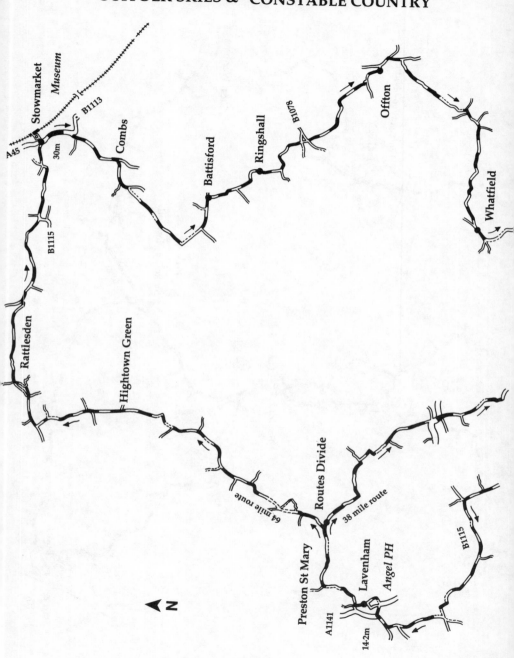

SUFFOLK - 16M ROUTE

0·0 LEFT out of Bures Village Hall.
Cycle 0·2m to T junction end.

0·2 RIGHT at T junction signposted High Street.
Cycle 0·1m to 1st right signposted Assington.

0·3 RIGHT signposted Assington. **Cycle 4·1m to T junction end with A134.**

4·4 RIGHT at T junction signposted Nayland 4. **Cycle 0·2m to 2nd left signposted 'Unsuitable for H.G.V.'**

4·6 LEFT signposted 'Unsuitable for H.G.V.'
Cycle 1·5m to T junction.

6·1 RIGHT at T junction signposted Stoke By Nayland.
Cycle 0·9m to T junction end.

The longer routes go left here – you turn right.

7·0 LEFT at T junction signposted Stoke By Nayland.
Cycle 2·2m to right turn in Stoke By Nayland, signposted Nayland.

9·2 RIGHT in Stoke By Nayland signposted Nayland.
Cycle 1·7m to T junction end.

10·9 RIGHT at T junction signposted Colchester.
Cycle 0·5m to crossroads end with A134.

11·4 CONT over crossroads with A134. **Cycle 4·3m to left turn into Bures Village Hall.**

15·7 LEFT into Bures Village Hall.

End of 16m route.

SUFFOLK - 38M ROUTE

0·0 LEFT out of Bures Village Hall. **Cycle 0·2m to T junction.**

0·2 RIGHT at T junction signposted High Street.
Cycle 0·1m to 1st right signposted Assington.

0·3 RIGHT signposted Assington. **Cycle 4·1m to T junction.**

4·4 RIGHT at T junction signposted Nayland 4. **Cycle 0·2m to 2nd left signposted 'Unsuitable for H.G.V.'**

4·6 LEFT signposted 'Unsuitable for H.G.V. '
Cycle 1·5m to T junction end.

6·1 LEFT at T junction signposted Boxford.
Cycle 0·8m to crossroads end.

The 16m route turns right here - you turn left.

6·9 CONT over unsignposted crossroads onto small path.
Cycle 0·1m to T junction end by Church.

7·0 RIGHT at T junction by church. **Cycle 0·1m to first left signposted Lavenham into Swan Street.**

7·1 LEFT signposted Lavenham into Swan Street.
Cycle 2·5m to T junction end.

9·6 RIGHT at T junction signposted Lavenham 6.
Cycle 0·1m to 1st left signposted Lavenham 4 ¾.

9·7 LEFT signposted Lavenham 4 ¾.
Cycle 1·9m to crossroads end.

11·6 LEFT at crossroads signposted Sudbury 6. **Cycle 1·1m to 1st right signposted Lavenham 2 ½.**

12·7 RIGHT signposted Lavenham 2 ½. **Cycle 1·5m to crossroads end.**

14·2 RIGHT at unsignposted T junction. **Cycle 1·8m through Lavenham to right turn at the edge of town signposted Preston 2 & Brettenham 4.**

16·0   RIGHT   signposted Preston 2. **Cycle 2m to right turn signposted Preston St Mary.**

18·0   RIGHT   signposted Preston St Mary. **Cycle 0·9m to 1st left signposted Monks Eleigh 2 ½.**

The 64m route continues here - you turn right.

18·9   LEFT   signposted Monks Eleigh 2 ½. **Cycle 0·7m to right turn signposted Monks Eleigh 1 ½.**

19·6   RIGHT   signposted Monks Eleigh 1 ½. **Cycle 1·6m to crossroads with A1141.**

21·2   CONT   over crossroads with A1141. **Cycle 0·1m to 1st right turn signposted Boxford.**

21·3   RIGHT   signposted Boxford. **Cycle 1·6m to T junction.**

22·9   RIGHT   at T junction signposted Boxford. **Cycle 1m to crossroads end.**

23·9   CONT   over crossroads signposted Boxford. **Cycle 0·5m to 1st unsignposted left turn.**

24·4   LEFT   unsignposted road. **Cycle 0·7m to 3rd right turn signposted Boxford.**

25·1   RIGHT   signposted Boxford. **Cycle 1·1m to grass triangle with tree in middle.**

26·2   LEFT   at grass triangle. **Cycle 0·6m to right turn just before Ash Street.**

26·8   RIGHT   unsignposted just before Ash Street. **Cycle 0·1m to T junction end.**

26·9   RIGHT   at unsignposted T junction. **Cycle 0·2m to left turn by large church signposted 'no through road.'**

27·1   LEFT   by large church signposted 'no through road'. **Cycle 0·2 to crossroads end with A1071.**

27·3   CONT   over crossroads (with A1071) signposted 'unsuitable for H.G.V.' **Cycle 1·7m to T junction end.**

29·0 LEFT at T junction signposted Stoke By Nayland 2. **Cycle 1·2m to right turn signposted Nayland.**

31·2 RIGHT in Stoke By Nayland signposted Nayland. **Cycle 1·7m to T junction end.**

32·9 RIGHT at T junction signposted Colchester. **Cycle 0·5m to crossroads end.**

33·4 CONT over crossroads with A134. **Cycle 4·3m to left turn into Bures Village Hall**

37·7 LEFT into Bures Village Hall.

End of 38m route.

SUFFOLK - 64 MILE ROUTE

0·0 LEFT out of Bures Village Hall. **Cycle 0·2m to T junction.**

0·2 RIGHT at T junction signposted High Street. **Cycle 0·1m to 1st right turn signposted Assington.**

0·3 RIGHT signposted Assington.
Cycle 4·1m to T junction end.

4·4 RIGHT at T junction signposted Nayland 4. **Cycle 0·2m to 2nd left signposted 'Unsuitable for H.G.V.'**

4·6 LEFT signposted 'Unsuitable for H.G.V.'
Cycle 1·5m to T junction end.

6·1 LEFT at T junction signposted Boxford.
Cycle 0·8m to crossroads end.

The 16m route goes right here - you turn left.

6·9 CONT over unsignposted crossroads onto small path.
Cycle 0·1m to T junction end by Church.

7·0 RIGHT at T junction by church. **Cycle 0·1m to 1st left signposted Lavenham into Swan Street.**

7·1 LEFT signposted Lavenham into Swan Street.
Cycle 2·5m to T junction end.

9·6 RIGHT at T junction signposted Lavenham 6.
Cycle 0·1m to 1st left signposted Lavenham 4 ¾.

9·7 LEFT signposted Lavenham 4 ¾.
Cycle 1·9m to crossroads end.

11·6 LEFT at crossroads signposted Sudbury 6. **Cycle 1·1m to 1st right signposted Lavenham 2 ½.**

12·7 RIGHT signposted Lavenham 2 ½.
Cycle 1·5m to crossroads end.

14·2 RIGHT at unsignposted T junction. **Cycle 1·8m through Lavenham to right turn just at the end of town signposted Preston 2 & Brettenham 4.**

16·0 RIGHT signposted Preston 2 & Brettenham 4.
Cycle 8·2m to T junction end.

18·0 *The 38m route turns right here - you continue.*

24·2 RIGHT at T junction signposted Stowmarket 5.
Cycle 2·6m to T junction end.

26·8 RIGHT at T junction signposted Stowmarket.
Cycle 1·7m to T junction end.

28·5 LEFT at T junction signposted Stowmarket.
Cycle 0·5m to traffic lights in Stowmarket centre.

30·0 RIGHT at traffic lights in Stowmarket onto A1308. (Walk bike
through no entry). **Cycle 0·6m to right turn
signposted Combs by Esso Petrol Station.**

30·6 RIGHT signposted Combs by petrol station.
Cycle 0·1m to 2nd left signposted Finsborough.

30·7 LEFT signposted Finsborough by barbers. **Cycle 4·2m
through Battisford to right signposted Ringshall 2.**

34·9 RIGHT signposted Ringshall 2. **Cycle 2·4m to crossroads.**

37·3 CONT over crossroads signposted Great Brickett.
Cycle 0·1m to crossroads end.

37·4 CONT over unsignposted crossroads by country furniture
house. **Cycle 1·7m to T junction end.**

39·1 LEFT at unsignposted T junction.
Cycle 0·4m to T junction end.

39·5 RIGHT at T junction signposted Somerham.
Cycle 0·3m to 1st right turn.

39·8 RIGHT into unsignposted road. **Cycle 4·2m through
Elmsett to T junction end.**

44·0 LEFT at T junction signposted Hadleigh 3.
Cycle 2·3m to crossroads end.

46·3   CONT   over crossroads with A1071 signposted Hadleigh.
Cycle 0·3m to T junction end.

46·6   LEFT   at unsignposted T junction in Hadleigh. **Cycle 0·4m
up Hadleigh high street to T junction end.**

47·0   LEFT   at unsignposted T junction into Station Road.
Cycle 1·8m to 2nd right by Kates Hill House.

48·8   RIGHT   by Kates Hill House. **Cycle 1m to T junction end.**

49·8   RIGHT   at unsignposted T junction. **Cycle 0·8m to 1st left
signposted Capel St Mary.**

50·6   LEFT   signposted Capel St Mary. **Cycle 1m to T junction.**

51·6   RIGHT   at T junction signposted Capel St Mary.
Cycle 0·6m to T junction end.

52·2   LEFT   at T junction signposted Colchester.
Cycle 0·4m to 1st right turn signposted Higham.

52·6   RIGHT   signposted Higham. **Cycle 0·1m to 1st
unsignposted left by grass triangle.**

52·7   LEFT   unsignposted by grass triangle.
Cycle 1m to T junction end.

53·7   RIGHT   at T junction signposted Stoke By Nayland 4.
**Cycle 4·1m to left turn in Stoke By Nayland
signposted Nayland.**

57·8   LEFT   in Stoke By Nayland signposted Nayland.
Cycle 1·7m to T junction end.

59·5   RIGHT   at T junction signposted Colchester.
Cycle 0·5m to crossroads end

60·0   CONT   over crossroads with A134. **Cycle 4·3m to left
turn into Bures Village Hall.**

64·3   LEFT   into Bures Village Hall.

End of 64m route.

THE NORTH DOWNS & SURREY HILLS

Two demanding excursions either side of the North Downs. The start point is close to Horsley Station where there is ample parking for cars. The short route restricts itself to the north side of the Downs and crosses through Effingham Forest under the North Downs Way.

The long route passes through Shere and heads south to Cranleigh. From here the hills begin in earnest as the route zig-zags through beautiful woodland to Peaslake, Holmbury St Mary and to Friday Street in the midst of National Trust land. The countryside here has a timeless quality and apart from the advent of tarmac it feels unspoilt and little changed over time.

The lanes in this area are a real feature of this ride and at times the exposed tree roots on the banks of the sunken tracks appear to be as old as the Mesolithic Dwelling site in Abinger Hammer. The road back towards Effingham over the North Downs Way offers a stiff climb up but a pleasing descent is the reward on the other side.

Map	OS LR 187 Dorking, Reigate & Crawley.
Distance	19 or 41 miles.
Start/Finish	East Horsley Village Hall, Kingston Avenue.

Railway Access

Horsley & Effingham Junction - trains from London Waterloo via Clapham Junction. Also from Guildford.

Gomshall - just off centre of route, trains from East Croydon via Redhill and also from Guildford.

Places to see

Silent Pool, Shere. This pond, surrounded by trees, is fed by a spring and legend has it that King John watched a local girl bathing here - it is said that the unfortunate damsel drowned herself in a fit of shame.

Shere. An attractive village which is very busy on sunny weekends.

Leith Hill. A National Trust site and 18th century tower. At 965 feet there are spectacular views over the North Downs and surrounding countryside. It is less than a mile from the route - if you can take on another hill!

Polesden Lacy. A beautiful Regency house high on the North Downs, with 1000 acres of grounds. Owned by the National Trust. Just over 1m off the route.

Hills & Woods. The lanes, hills and woods on this route, particularly around Holmbury, Abinger Common and Friday Street are well worth exploring. Trees overhang the narrow lanes to form a dark canopy over the sunken lanes and you feel a long way from the hustle & bustle of south-east England.

Tourist Information Office, High Street, Guildford 0483 444007.

Refreshments

White Horse PH & Astor's Tea House, Shere - 6.4m.

Onslow Arms PH, High Street, Cranleigh - 13.8m.

Hurtwood PH, Peaslake - 21.4m.

Stephen Langton PH, Friday Street - 27m.

Abinger Hatch Pub, Abinger Common - 28.5m.

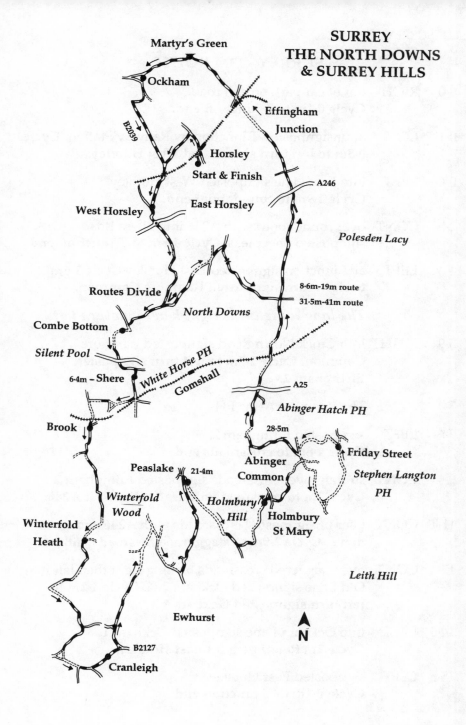

SURREY
THE NORTH DOWNS
& SURREY HILLS

SURREY - 19M ROUTE

0·0   RIGHT out of car park on exit road.
       Cycle 0·1m to T junction end.

0·1   LEFT   at unsignposted T junction by Railway Station. **Cycle 0·5m to left turn signposted West Horsley.**

0·6   LEFT   into East Lane signposted West Horsley.
       Cycle 1·9m to roundabout end.

2·5   CONT   over roundabout with A246 into Shere Road signposted Sheepleas. **Cycle 1·8m to T junction end.**

4·3   LEFT   at T junction signposted East Horsley.**Cycle 1·6m to right turn signposted Ranmore Common.**

The long route turns right here- you turn left.

5·9   RIGHT into Crock North Road signposted Ranmore Common. **Cycle 1·7m to left turn signposted Effingham 2.**

7·4   The Ranmore Arms PH.

7·6   LEFT   signposted Effingham 2.
       Cycle 1·8m to crossroads end.

9·4   CONT   straight over crossroads signposted Effingham 2. **Cycle 2m to crossroad with traffic lights at A246.**

11·4   CONT   over unsignposted crossroads with A246 and traffic lights. **Cycle 2·0m to staggered crossroads end.**

13·4   CONT   over staggered crossroads turning right then left into Old Lane signposted Ockham 2 ¼. **Cycle 1·2m to left turn signposted Ockham 1.**

14·6   LEFT   into Ockham Lane signposted Ockham 1.
       Cycle 1m to left turn for East Horsley.

15·6   LEFT   signposted East Horsley.
       Cycle 0·1m to T junction end.

15·7 LEFT   at T junction signposted East Horsley. **Cycle 0·1m to right turn on bend signposted West Horsley.**

15·8   RIGHT on bend signposted West Horsley. **Cycle 1·7m to T junction.**

17·5   LEFT   at T junction into The Street signposted East Horsley. **Cycle 0·7m to T juncion end.**

18·2   RIGHT at T junction onto B2039 signposted East Horsley. **Cycle 0·4m to right turn after railway bridge.**

18·6   RIGHT into Kingston Avenue just before shops signposted Medical Centre. **Cycle 0·2m to end.**

18·8   Arrive back at Hall.

End of 19M Route.

SURREY - 41 MILE ROUTE

0·0 CONT out of car park towards Station. **Cycle 0·1m to T junction end.**

0·1 LEFT unsignposted at station. **Cycle 0·5m to left turn signposted West Horsley**

0·6 LEFT into East Lane signposted West Horsley. **Cycle 1·9m to roundabout.**

2·5 CONT at roundabout with A246 into Shere Road signposted Sheepleas ½. **Cycle 2·8m to T junction end.**

4·3 RIGHT at T junction signposted Shere. **Cycle 1·7m to staggered crossroads end with the A25.**

The short route turns left here.

6·0 CONT over staggered crossroads into Upper Street signposted Shere. **Cycle 0·4m to right turn by 'Antique & Gifts' shop in Shere.**

6·4 RIGHT in Shere by 'Antique & Gifts'. **Cycle 0·6m uphill to right turn just before rail bridge signposted Farley Green & Aldbury.**

7·0 RIGHT just before railway bridge signposted Farley Green & Aldbury. **Cycle 0·9m to T junction end.**

7·9 LEFT at T junction into New Road signposted Farley Green. **Cycle 1m to left turn signposted Smithwood Common & Cranleigh.**

8·9 LEFT into signposted Smithwood Common, Cranleigh & Shophouse Lane. **Cycle 0·4m to right turn signposted Winterfold.**

10·3 RIGHT signposted Winterfold. **Cycle 2·7m to T junction.**

12·0 LEFT at T junction signposted Cranleigh School. **Cycle 1·8 to T junction.**

13·8 LEFT at T junction signposted Horsham B2128.

Cycle 0·5m through Cranleigh to roundabout.

14·3 LEFT at roundabout signposted Ewehurst 2. **Cycle 0·7m
to left turn signposted Albury 6, Shere 5 & Barhatch
Road.**

15·0 LEFT at Barnhatch Road signposted Albury 6.
Cycle 2·4m to T junction.

17·4 RIGHT at T junction signposted Ewehurst. **Cycle 1m to
left turn on steep descent signposted Shere 2 ½
Aldbury.**

18·4 LEFT signposted Shere 2 ½ & Aldbury. **Cycle 2m to right
turn into Radnor Road by stone War Memorial in
middle of the road.**

20·4 RIGHT by stone War Memorial in Peaslake into Radnor
Road. **Cycle 1·7m to left turn on sharp descent
signed Holmbury & Dorking**

22·1 LEFT signposted Holmbury, Dorking. **Cycle 1·3m to
staggered crossroads.**

23·4 CONT over staggered crossroads (right then left) signposted
Common Leith Hill. **Cycle 1·1m to T junction .**

24·5 RIGHT at T junction signposted Leith Hill.
Cycle 1·1m to left turn signposted Broadmoor.

25·6 LEFT signposted Broadmoor. **Cycle 1·3m to left turn
into Friday Street.**

26·9 LEFT into Friday Street. **Cycle 1m to T junction end.**

27·9 LEFT at T junction. **Cycle 0·1m to right turn signposted
Abinger Hammer.**

28·0 RIGHT signposted Abinger Hammer. **Cycle 1·5m to
T junction end.**

28·5 Abinger Hatch PH

29·5 RIGHT at unsignposted T junction. **Cycle 0·2m to
crossroads end with A25.**

29·7 CONT over A25 signposted Effingham. **Cycle1·8m to crossroads end.**

31·5 CONT at crossroads signposted Effingham 2. **Cycle 2 m to crossroads end.**

The 20 mile route rejoins you here.

33·5 CONT over crossroads with A246 & traffic lights. **Cycle 2m to crossroads end.**

35·5 CONT over staggered crossroads (right then left) signposted Ockham 2 ¼ . **Cycle 1·2m to left turn signposted Ockham 1.**

36·7 LEFT into Ockham Lane signposted Ockham 1, Ripley & Wisley. **Cycle 1m to left turn signposted East Horsley by PH.**

37·7 LEFT signposted East Horsley. **Cycle 0·1m to T junction.**

37·8 LEFT at T junction signposted East Horsley, West Horsley. **Cycle 0·2m to first right turn on bend signposted West Horsley.**

38·0 RIGHT signposted West Horsley. **Cycle 1·7m to T junction end.**

39·7 LEFT at T junction signposted East Horsley. **Cycle 0·7m to T junction end.**

40·4 RIGHT at T junction signposted East Horsley. **Cycle 0·4m to right turn after railway bridge signposted Medical Centre, by shops**.

40·8 RIGHT signposted Medical Centre. **Cycle 0·2m to Hall.**

41·0 Arrive back at Hall.

End of 41 mile route.

THE LONG MAN, THE DOWNS & THE WEALD

The Long Man of Wilmington

Two different routes of 38m and 50m starting in the county town of Lewes. Both routes head east towards Ringmer then turn south past Glyndeborne, through Glynde, across the river to the South Downs. The route passes Arlington Reservoir and continues south along the Cuckmere River Valley to Alfriston, considered to be one of the most attractive villages in Sussex.

A climb follows over the South Downs Way and alongside The Long Man of Wilmington to head towards Lower Dicker past the remains of Michelham Priory. The routes divide at Muddles Green where the 38m route heads back to Lewes and the 50m route continues north into the Sussex Weald between Heathfield and Uckfield.

This route is very adaptable and for instance it would be easy to miss the loop to Alfriston and the climbs over the Downs to head straight to Muddles Green where the two routes divide.

Map	OS LR 198 Brighton & the Downs.
	OS LR 199 Eastbourne & Hastings.
Distance	38 or 48 miles.
Start/Finish	All Saints Art Centre, Lewes.

Railway Access

Uckfield - north on the route, trains from Victoria via East Croydon.

Lewes & Polegate - trains from London Victoria and from Brighton & Hastings along the south coast.

Places to see

Lewes. Attractions include the Norman Castle, Anne of Cleeve's House and the gardens at Southover Grange.

Glynde Place. Built in 1579, the home of Viscount Hampden is open to visitors.

Firle Place. A large country house and home of the Gage family for 500 years. It is set in lovely parkland below the backdrop of Firle Beacon.

Charleston Farmhouse. 1m off the route, off the A27. This charming farmhouse was once the home of Bloomsbury artists Vanessa and Clive Bell and Duncan Grant and has been preserved in true Bloomsbury style.

Alfriston. An attractive village with the 13th century Star Inn, the 14th century Clergy House and a heritage centre.

Michelham Priory, Upper Dicker. A 13th century priory in 6 acres of gardens with many attractions including a Psychic Garden and a working Watermill. Also a tea room.

St Georges Vineyard, Waldron. a family run vineyard of 20 acres in an ancient estate. Tours, wine and teas.

Bentley Wildfowl & Motor Museum. Wildfowl, motor cars, art & antiques in a Country House with formal gardens.

Tourist Information Office, High Street, Lewes 0273 483448.

Refreshments

Tea rooms & shop, Firle Place - 33m, short route.

Star Inn & Ye Olde Smugglers Inne & tea shops, Alfriston - 14.8m.

The Star Inn, Waldron - 30.1m, 48m route.

Tea rooms, Bentley Wildfowl Trust - 40.3m.

SUSSEX
THE LONG MAN, THE DOWNS & THE WEALD

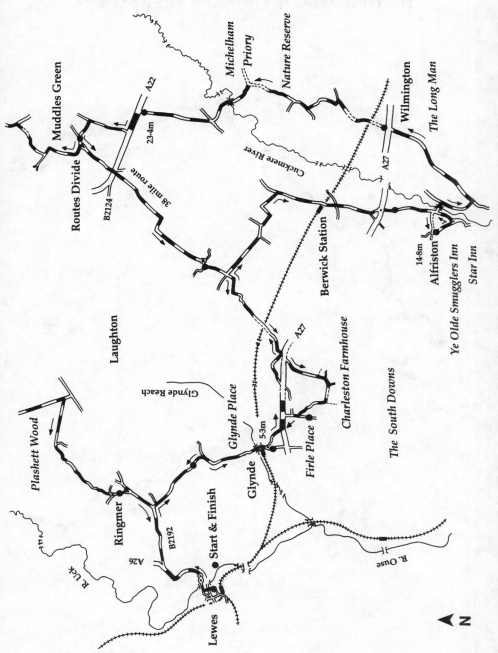

Muddles Green

A22

Michelham Priory

Nature Reserve

Wilmington

The Long Man

Routes Divide

23·4m

B2124

38 mile route

Cuckmere River

A27

Laughton

Berwick Station

14·8m

Alfriston

Ye Olde Smugglers Inn

Star Inn

Glynde Reach

Glynde Place

A27

Charleston Farmhouse

The South Downs

Plashett Wood

5·3m

Firle Place

Ringmer

Glynde

B2192

Start & Finish

A26

R. Uck

Lewes

R. Ouse

N

SUSSEX
THE LONG MAN, THE DOWNS & THE WEALD

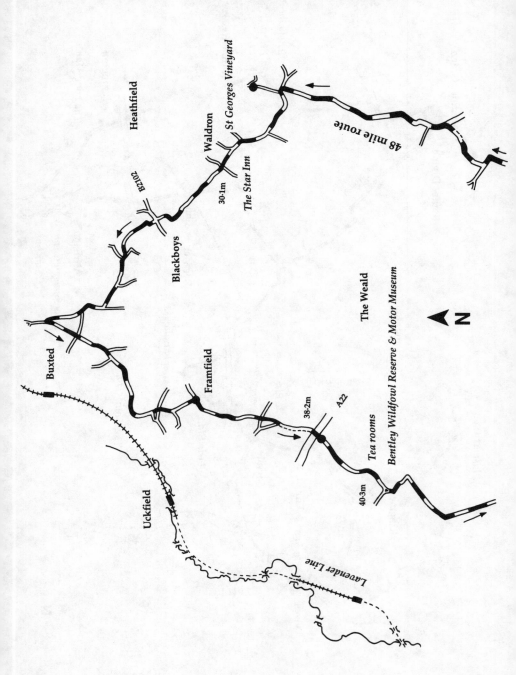

Heathfield

St Georges Vineyard

Waldron

B2102

30·1m

The Star Inn

Blackboys

48 mile route

Buxted

Framfield

The Weald

Bentley Wildfowl Reserve & Motor Museum

N

Uckfield

38·2m

A22

Tea rooms

40·3m

Lavender Line

SUSSEX - 38M ROUTE

0·0   RIGHT   out of All Saints Art Centre. **Cycle 200 yards to crossroads by Lansdown PH.**

0·1   RIGHT   at crossroads into Station Road. **Cycle 0·1m up to the traffic lights.**

0·2   CONT   over these traffic lights into Fisher Street. **Cycle 0·1m to T junction by Police Station.**

0·3   RIGHT   at T junction by Police Station signposted A26. **Cycle 0·2m along the A26 to two roundabouts.**

0·5   CONT   over roundabouts on A26 signposted London. **Cycle 0·7m to right turn signposted Ringmer B2192.**

1·2   RIGHT   signposted Ringmer B2192. **Cycle 1·5m to right turn signposted Glynde.**

2·8   RIGHT   signposted Glynde. **Cycle 2·5m to left turn opposite Trevor Arms PH by Glynde Railway station.**

5·3   LEFT   opposite Trevor Arms PH up unsignposted road. **Cycle 0·5m to T junction end.**

5·8   LEFT   onto unsignposted main road. **Cycle 0·8m to 2nd left turn by Birch Lane Cottages.**

6·6   LEFT   into unsignposted road by Birch Lane Cottages. **Cycle 0·7m to T junction end.**

7·3   LEFT   at unsignposted T junction. **Cycle 1·9m to crossroads signposted Berwick Station.**

9·2   RIGHT   at crossroads signposted Berwick Station 2 ½. **Cycle 0·9m to T junction.**

10·1   LEFT   at T junction signposted Berwick Station. **Cycle 0·2m to T junction end.**

10·3   RIGHT   at T junction signposted Berwick. **Cycle 0·9m to T junction end.**

11·2 RIGHT at T junction signposted Alfriston 3 ½.
Cycle 1·8m to roundabout.

13·0 CONT over roundabout signposted Alfriston. **Cycle 1m to 1st right turn into Wilton Street.**

14·0 RIGHT into Wilton Street. **Cycle 0·4m to unsignposted left turn at the top of the road.**

14·4 LEFT at top of road into an unsignposted road. **Cycle 0·4m down to a T junction in Alfriston Village.**

14·8 LEFT at T junction in village centre into road with tiny Bus Parking signpost. **Cycle 0·4m to 1st right turn signposted Litlington.**

15·2 RIGHT signposted Litlington. **Cycle 0·8m to T junction.**

16·0 LEFT at T junction signposted Wilmington. **Cycle 2·1m to crossroads end.**

17·5 CONT passing car park for The Long Man & Wilmington Priory.

18·1 CONT over A27 into Thornwell Road. **Cycle 1·3m to T junction end.**

19·4 RIGHT at T junction signposted Upper Dicker 2 ¼. **Cycle 1m to T junction end.**

20·4 LEFT at T junction signposted Upper Dicker 1. **Cycle 0·7m to staggered crossroads end.**

21·1 CONT at staggered crossroads by school into Camberlot Road. **Cycle to T junction end with A22.**

23·3 LEFT at T junction onto A22. **Cycle 0·5m to right turn signposted Gunhill.**

23·8 RIGHT signposted Gunhill. **Cycle 0·8m to 1st left signposted Golden Cross.**

24·6 LEFT signposted Golden Cross 1 ¼. **Cycle 0·6m to 1st left turn signposted Golden Cross ¾.**

25·2   LEFT   signposted Golden Cross ¾. **Cycle 0·7m to crossroads with A22.**

25·9   CONT   over A22 taking footpath on the left hand side of the PH which joins the road to Ripe. **Cycle 2·4m to roundabout end.**

28·3   CONT   through roundabout signposted Lewes. **Cycle 2·6m to an unsignposted right turn just before A27.**

31·0   RIGHT   down unsignposted road just before A27. **Cycle 0·6m to staggered crossroads end.**

31·6   CONT   over staggered crossroads signposted Firle Place 1 ¼. **Cycle 0·6m to T junction end.**

32·2   RIGHT   at T junction unsignposted. **Cycle 0·2m to T junction with A27.**

32·4   LEFT   at T junction with A27. **Cycle 0·2m to unsignposted right turn by Q8 garage.**

32·6   RIGHT   by Q8 garage into unsignposted road. **Cycle 0·6m to T junction end.**

33·2   RIGHT   at T junction opposite Trevor Arms PH. **Cycle 2·6m to T junction end.**

35·8   LEFT   at T junction signposted Lewes 2 ½. **Cycle 1·2m to T junction end.**

37·0   LEFT   at T junction signposted Lewes. **Cycle 0·7m to twin roundabouts.**

37·7   CONT   over twin roundabouts signposted Town Centre. **Cycle 0·3m into town.**

38·0   CONT   follow signs for British Rail into Friars Walk. **Cycle 0·3m back to All Saints Art Centre.**

38·3   back at All Saints Art Centre.

End of 38m route.

SUSSEX - 48 MILE ROUTE

0·0   RIGHT out of All Saints Art Centre. **Cycle 200 yards to crossroads by Lansdown PH.**

0·1   RIGHT at crossroads into Station Road.
Cycle 0·1m to traffic lights.

0·2   CONT at traffic lights into Fisher Street. **Cycle 0·1m to T junction by Police Station.**

0·3   RIGHT at T junction by Police Station signposted A26.
Cycle 0·2m along A26 to twin roundabouts.

0·5   CONT at twin roundabouts on A26 signposted London.
Cycle 0·7m to right turn for Ringmer B2192.

1·2   RIGHT signposted Ringmer B2192. **Cycle 1·5m to right turn signposted Glynde.**

2·8   RIGHT signposted Glynde. **Cycle for 2·5m to Trevor Arms PH near Glynde Railway Station.**

5·3   LEFT opposite Trevor Arms PH up unsignposted road.
Cycle 0·5m to T junction end.

5·8   LEFT onto unsignposted main road. **Cycle 0·8m to 2nd left turn by Birch Lane Cottages.**

6·6   LEFT into unsignposted road by Birch Lane Cottages.
Cycle 0·7m to T junction end.

7·3   LEFT at unsignposted T junction.
Cycle 1·9m to crossroads end.

9·2   RIGHT at crossroads signposted Berwick Station 2 ½.
Cycle 0·9m to T junction end.

10·1   LEFT at T junction signposted Berwick Station.
Cycle 0·2m to T junction end.

10·3   RIGHT signposted Berwick. **Cycle 0·9m to T junction end.**

11·2   RIGHT at T junction signposted Alfriston 3 ½.

Cycle 1·8m to roundabout.

13·0 CONT over roundabout signposted Alfriston. **Cycle 1m to 1st right turn into Wilton Street.**

14·0 RIGHT into Wilton Street. **Cycle 0·4m to unsignposted left turn at the top of the road.**

14·4 LEFT at top of road into an unsignposted road. **Cycle 0·4m down to a T junction in Alfriston Village.**

14·8 LEFT at T junction in village centre up road with tiny Bus Parking signpost. **Cycle 0·4m to 1st right turn signposted Litlington.**

15·2 RIGHT signposted Litlington. **Cycle 0·8m to T junction.**

16·0 LEFT at T junction signposted Wilmington. **Cycle 2·1m to crossroads end.**

17·5 CONT passing car park for The Long Man & Wilmington Priory.

18·1 CONT over A27 into Thornwell Road. **Cycle 1·3m to T junction end.**

19·4 RIGHT at T junction signposted Upper Dicker 2 ¼. **Cycle 1m T junction to end.**

20·4 LEFT at T junction signposted Upper Dicker 1. **Cycle 0·7m to staggered crossroads to end.**

21·1 CONT at staggered crossroads by school into Camberlot Road. **Cycle to T junction end with A22.**

23·3 LEFT at T junction onto A22. **Cycle 0·5m to right turn signposted Gunhill.**

23·8 RIGHT signposted Gunhill. **Cycle 0·8m to 1st left signposted Golden Cross.**

24·6 LEFT signposted Golden Cross 1 ¼. **Cycle 1·3m to right turn signposted Horam 3.**

25·9 RIGHT signposted Horam 3. **Cycle 0·9m to grass triangle.**

26·8   LEFT   at unsignposted grass triangle.
Cycle 0·2m to next grass triangle.

27·0   RIGHT   at grass triangle signposted Waldron.
Cycle 2·0m to T junction end.

29·0   LEFT   at T junction signposted Waldron 1. **Cycle 1·1m to War Memorial in Waldron.**

30·1   CONT   to left in Waldron by War Memorial.
Recommended lunch stop - The Star Inn.
Cycle 0·5m to crossroads end.

30·5   CONT   over crossroads signposted Blackboys.
Cycle 1·3m to staggered crossroads end.

31·8   CONT   over staggered crossroads signposted Pottery.
Cycle 0·7m to T junction end.

32·5   RIGHT   at unsignposted T junction. **Cycle 1·7m to T junction end.**

33·4   CONT   to right on downhill signposted Buxted at grass triangle.

33·7   CONT   signposted Hadlow Down.

34·2   LEFT   at T junction signposted Framfield 2 ½.
Cycle 2·4m to T junction end.

36·6   LEFT   at T junction signposted B2102. **Cycle 0·3m to 1st right turn signposted Halland 2 ¾.**

37·0   RIGHT   signposted Halland 2 ¾. **Cycle 0·9m to crossroads.**

37·9   CONT   over crossroads signposted Halland 1 ¾.
Cycle 0·3m to T junction end.

38·2   LEFT   at T junction signposted A22. **Cycle 0·5m to end.**

38·7   CONT   over A22 at staggered crossroads signposted Bentley Wildfowl & Motor Museum 1 ½. **Cycle 1·3m to 1st left signposted Bentley.**

40·0   LEFT   signposted Bentley. **Cycle to immediate T junction.**

40·0 LEFT at unsignposted T junction. **Cycle 2m to a right turn signposted Green Lane.**

40·3 CONT pass Bentley Wildfowl trust (Tea rooms inside).

42·0 RIGHT signposted Green Lane. **Cycle 2·3m to T junction.**

44·3 LEFT at T junction signposted Ringmer. **Cycle 0·2m to T junction end.**

44·5 RIGHT at T junction signposted Lewes 2. **Cycle 1·9m to T junction end.**

46·4 LEFT at T junction signposted Lewes A26. **Cycle 0·7m to twin roundabouts.**

47·0 CONT over twin roundabouts signposted Town Centre. **Cycle 0·3m into town.**

47·3 CONT follow signs for Railway Station into Friars Walk. **Cycle 0·3m back to All Saints Art Centre.**

47·7 ARRIVE back at All Saints Art Centre.

End of 50m route.

FOSSE WAY, STRATFORD & THE OXFORD CANAL

The start point for this ride is at Wolston, 5m east of Coventry, although Stratford would be one of many alternative access points. The routes cover a figure of eight encircling Stratford-Upon-Avon in one half of the eight and Southam in the other. The Fosse Way Roman Road forms the backbone of the ride and can easily be used as a reference point for varying the route.

At 50m and 90m the routes might appear to be long, but as 22 miles can be covered on the straight-as-an-arrow Fosse Way the miles are covered quickly with a minimum of map reading. Off the Roman Road, the cycling is on minor roads and narrow lanes, and offers great variety with open countryside and a number of demanding hills to keep the legs working.

The 50m leg restricts itself to the first half of the figure of eight and crosses both the Oxford and Grand Union canal to rejoin the Fosse Way at Princethorpe. The 90m route takes in a clockwise circuit of Stratford and passes through a number of attractive villages.

Map	OS LR 140 Leicester & Coventry, 151 Stratford.
Distance	50 or 90 miles.
Start/Finish	Brandon & Wolston Village Hall, Main Street.

Railway Access

Coventry - main line from Euston and Birmingham.

Stratford Upon-Avon - trains from Birmingham.

Leamington Spa - from the south via Banbury and from Birmingham and Coventry to the north.

Places to see

Stratford-Upon-Avon. Shakespeare, Anne Hathaway's Cottage and olde England. Despite the hordes of summer visitors it is still worth a detour. It is possible to take a cycle path, a disused railway, from Long Marston to cover the 4m cross country to Stratford. It would then be easy to take the B4086 out of Statford to rejoin the route near Wellesbourne.

Charlecote Park, near Wellesbourne. An Elizabethan house, a National Trust property, with 19th century additions.

The Oxford Canal. Between Chapel Green and Marston Doles, 1m off the route, there is a host of locks and a canal-side tow path which make for excellent boat watching.

Draycote Water Country Park. A popular park and picnic spot overlooking the reservoir. Located 1.5m off the route.

Tourist Information Office, Jury Street, Warwick 0926 492212.

Refreshments

Pub, Wharf (next to Oxford Canal) - 27.3m, 50m. 67m, 90m.

White Bear PH & shops, Shipston-on-Stour - 25.9m, long route.

Howard Arms PH, Ilmington - 29.6m, long route.

Blue Boar PH, Long Marston - 40.9m, long route.

Shops, Wellesbourne - 53.8m, long route.

WARWICKSHIRE
FOSSE WAY, STRATFORD & THE OXFORD CANAL

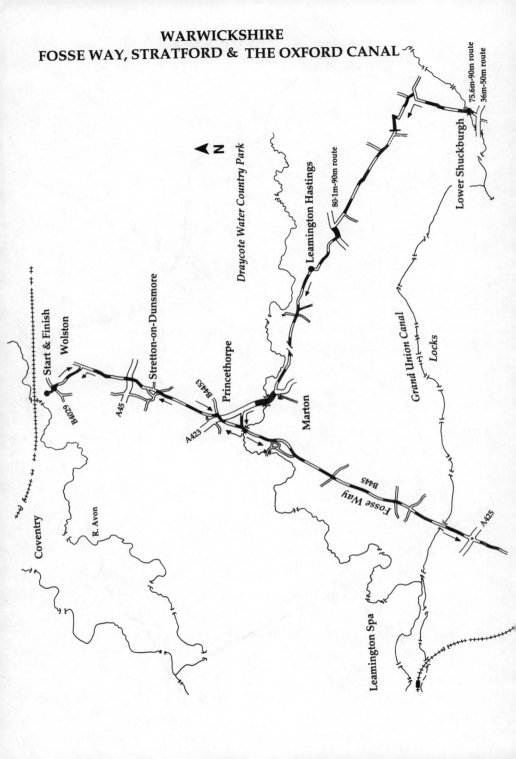

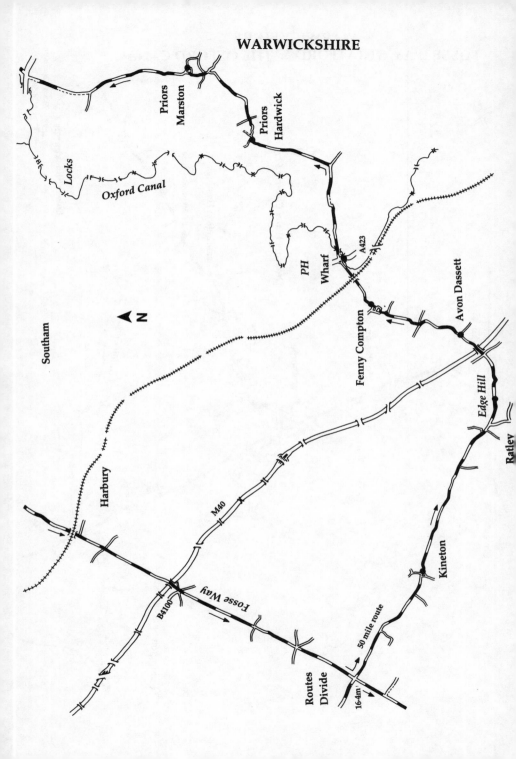

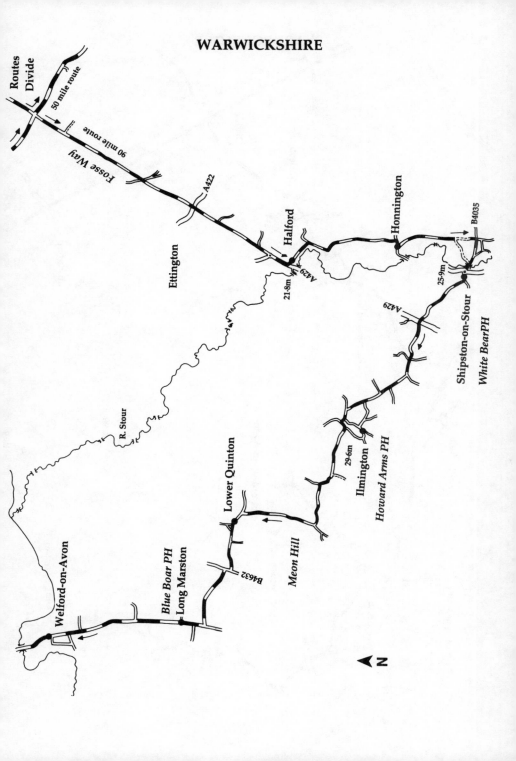

WARWICKSHIRE

Routes Divide

50 mile route

90 mile route

Fosse Way

A422

Ettington

Halford

21·8m

A429

Honnington

25·9m

A429

B4035

Shipston-on-Stour

White Bear PH

R. Stour

Lower Quinton

Ilmington

29·6m

Howard Arms PH

Meon Hill

Welford-on-Avon

Blue Boar PH

Long Marston

B4632

N

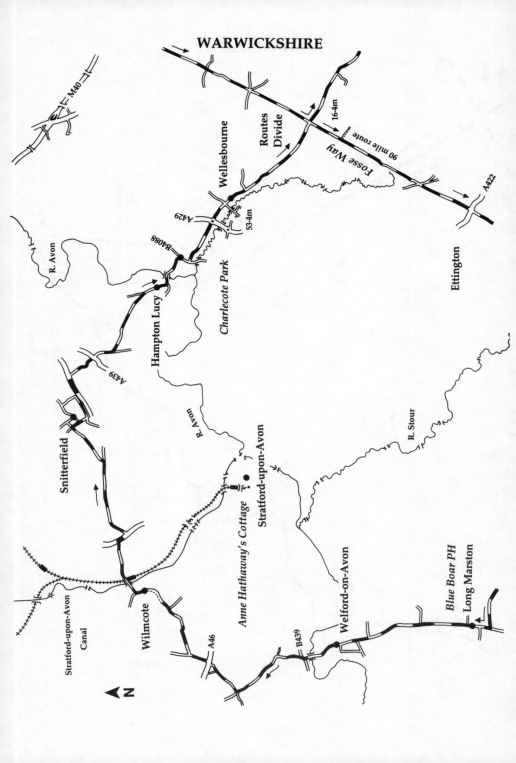

WARWICKSHIRE - 50 MILE ROUTE

0·0   LEFT   out of Brandon Village Hall. **Cycle 0·2m to T junction in village by shops.**

0·2   CONT   over staggered crossroads and into Dyers Way in front of you. **Cycle 0·8m to T junction end.**

1·0   RIGHT   at unsignposted T junction onto the Fosse Way. **Cycle 0·8m to roundabout end.**

1·8   CONT   over roundabout signposted B4455 Cirencester Fosse Way. **Cycle 1·8m to T junction end.**

3·6   RIGHT   at T junction signposted Leamington & Cirencester. **Cycle 0·1m to staggered crossroads end.**

3·7   CONT   over staggered crossroads signposted Stow & Fosse Way. **Cycle 2·4m to crossroads end.**

6·1   CONT   over crossroads signposted Cirencester & Fosse Way. **Cycle 2·8m to roundabout end with A425.**

8·9   CONT   over roundabout signposted Cirencester & Fosse Way. **Cycle 3·8m to roundabout end.**

12·7   CONT   over roundabout signposted Stow, Cirencester & Fosse Way. **Cycle 3·7m to crossroads end.**

The 90m route continues at this junction.

16·4   LEFT   at crossroads signposted Kineton & Banbury B4086. **Cycle 2·4m to T junction end in Kineton.**

18·8   RIGHT   at T junction in Kineton. **Cycle 3·2m along B4086 to left turn for Arlescotte ½ & Avon Dasset 2.**

22·0   LEFT   signposted Arlescotte ½ & Avon Dasset 2. **Cycle 1·6m to crossroads end with B4100.**

23·6   CONT   over crossroads signposted Avon Dasset ½ & Farnborough 2 ¼. **Cycle 2·5m through Avon Dasset to T junction in Fenny Compton.**

26·1 RIGHT at T junction signposted Wormleighton 2.
Cycle 0·1m to T junction end.

26·2 LEFT signposted Wormleighton 2. **Cycle 1·1m to staggered crossroads end with A423.**

27·3 CONT (right then left) over staggered crossroads signposted Wormleighton 1 & Priors Hardwick 3. **Cycle 2m through Wormleighton to left turn signposted Priors Hardwick 1 ½.**

29·3 LEFT signposted Priors Hardwick 1 ½. **Cycle 3·1m via Priors Hardwick to T junction in PriorsMarston.**

32·4 LEFT at T junction signposted Lower Shuckburgh 3. **Cycle 0·1m to 2nd right by memorial ahead signposted Lower Shuckburgh 3.**

32·5 RIGHT bymemorial signposted Lower Shuckburgh 3. **Cycle 2·3m to right turn signposted Lower Shuckburgh.**

34·8 RIGHT signposted Lower Shuckburgh 1 ¼. **Cycle 1·2m to staggered crossroads end with A425. Caution - gated road - 5 gates in all.**

36·0 CONT (right then left) over staggered crossroads signposted Willoughby 3. **Cycle 1·4m to left turn signposted Willoughby 2 ½ by a bridge over disused railway.**

37·4 LEFT signposted Willoughby 2 ½ & over rail bridge. **Cycle to 1st left turn signposted Leamington Hastings.**

37·5 LEFT signposted Leamington Hastings 3 ¼ (gated road). **Cycle 3m to T junction end with A426.**

40·5 LEFT at T junction signposted A426 Banbury. **Cycle 0·2m to 1st right signposted Leamington Hastings & Birdingbury.**

40·7 RIGHT signposted Leamington Hastings & Birdingbury. **Cycle 3·3m through Leamington Hastings & Birdinbury to T junction with A423 in Marton.**

44·0 RIGHT at T junction inMarton signposted Coventry. **Cycle 0·7m to 1st left turn signposted Eathorpe 1 ¼.**

44·7 LEFT signposted Eathorpe 1 ¼. **Cycle 0·4m to T junction end with B4455 Fosse Way.**

45·1 RIGHT at T junction signposted B4455 Fosse Way & Princethorpe ½. **Cycle 0·4m to crossroads end.**

45·5 CONT over staggered crossroads signposted Leicester B4455 & Fosse Way. **Cycle 0·1m to 1st left turn signposted Leicester, Fosse Way & Stretton.**

45·6 LEFT signposted Leicester, Fosse Way & Stretton. **Cycle 1·8m to roundabout with A45.**

47·4 CONT over roundabout signposted Leicester Fosse Way. **Cycle 0·9m to left turn into Dyers Lane.**

48·3 LEFT signposted Dyers Lane. **Cycle 0·7m to crossroads end in Wolston - caution narrow road.**

49·0 CONT over crossroads in Wolston into road signposted Main Street. **Cycle 0·4m to Wolston village hall.**

50·4 CONT back into Wolston village hall.

End of 50m route.

WARWICKSHIRE - 90M ROUTE

0·0   LEFT   out of Brandon Village Hall. **Cycle 0·2m to T junction in village by shops.**

0·2   CONT   over staggered crossroads and into Dyers Way in front of you. **Cycle 0·8m to T junction end.**

1·0   RIGHT   at unsignposted T junction onto the Fosse Way. **Cycle 0·8m to roundabout end.**

1·8   CONT   over roundabout signposted B4455 Cirencester & Fosse Way. **Cycle 1·8m to T junction end.**

3·6   RIGHT   at T junction signposted Leamington & Cirencester. **Cycle 0·1m to staggered crossroads end.**

3·7   CONT   over staggered crossroads signposted Stow & Fosse Way. **Cycle 2·4m to crossroads end.**

6·1   CONT   over crossroads signposted Cirencester & Fosse Way. **Cycle 2·8m to roundabout end with A425.**

8·9   CONT   over roundabout signposted Cirencester & Fosse Way. **Cycle 3·8m to roundabout end.**

12·7   CONT   over roundabout signposted Stow, Cirencester & Fosse Way. **Cycle 3·7m to crossroads end.**

The 50m route turns left here.

16·4   CONT   over crossroads signposted B4455 Cirencester. **Cycle 3·4m to crossroads end with A422.**

19·8   CONT   over crossroads signposted B4455 Cirencester. **Cycle 1·6m to roundabout end with A429.**

21·4   CONT   over roundabout signposted Stow & Shipston. **Cycle 0·4m to 1st left turn signposted Idlicote.**

21·8   LEFT   signposted Ildicote. **Cycle 0·5m to first right turn signposted Honnington.**

22·3   RIGHT   signposted Honington. **Cycle 1·7m to T junction.**

24·0 RIGHT at T junction signposted Shipston. **Cycle 0·1m to left turn signposted Barcheston Willington.**

24·1 LEFT signposted Barcheston Willington. **Cycle 1·1m to first right turn signposted Shipton.**

25·2 RIGHT signposted Shipton. **Cycle 0·6m to T junction end.**

25·8 RIGHT into Shipston On Stour. **Cycle 0·1m to T junction end.**

25·9 RIGHT at T junction signposted Chipping Campden & Stratford. **Follow signs for B4040 Chipping Campden.**

30·0 LEFT signposted B4040 Chipping Campden. **Cycle 0·2m to right turn signposted Ilmington 3 ½.**

26·1 RIGHT signposted Ilmington 3 ½. **Cycle 1·2m to crossroads end with A429.**

27·3 CONT over crossroads signposted Illmimgton 2 ½. **Cycle 2·3m to T junction end.**

29·6 LEFT at T junction signposted Mickleton, Campden & Stratford. **Cycle 0·2m to T junction end.**

29·8 RIGHT at T junction signposted Adminton, Mickleton & Stratford. **Cycle 0·1m to 1st left turn.**

29·9 LEFT signposted Adminton 2 ½ & Mickleton 3 ¾. **Cycle 2·2m to right turn signposted Quinton Stratford 1 ½ & Stratford 9.**

30·0 RIGHT signposted Quinton 1 ½ & Stratford 9. **Cycle 3·4m to T junction end.**

33·4 LEFT at T junction signposted Quinton ¼ & Stratford 7. **Cycle 1·1m via Lower Quinton to T junction end.**

34·5 RIGHT at T junction signposted Long Marston & Stratford. **Cycle 0·2m to 1st left turn for Long Marston.**

34·7 LEFT signposted Long Marston 1 ½. **Cycle 1·2m to**

T junction end.

35·9 RIGHT at T junction. **Cycle 3·5m through Long Marston & Welford to T junction end with B469.**

39·4 CONT at staggered crossroads signposted Binton. **Cycle 1·5m to right turn Billesley 1 ¼ by Blue Boar PH.**

40·9 RIGHT by Blue Boar PH signposted Billesey 1 ¼. **Cycle 0·8m to crossroads end with A46.**

41·7 CONT over crossroads signposted Billesley ½. **Cycle 0·3m to first right turn signposted Wilmcote 1 ¾.**

42·0 RIGHT signposted Wilmcote 1 ¾. **Cycle 1·8m to right turn in Wilmcote signposted Stratford 4 & Henly 7.**

43·8 RIGHT signposted Stratford 4 & Henly 7. **Cycle 1·8m to T junction end with A3400.**

44·9 RIGHT at T junction signposted Stratford 2. **Cycle 0·2m to 1st left turn signposted Snitterfield 2 ½.**

45·1 LEFT signposted Snitterfield 2 ½. **Cycle 1·5m to 1st left turn signposted Snitterfield ¾ & Green Rd.**

46·6 LEFT signposted Snitterfield ¾ & Green Road. **Cycle 0·9m to crossroads end.**

47·5 RIGHT opposite the Foxhunter PH signposted Stratford 4 & Warwick 5. **Cycle 0·7m to T junction end.**

48·2 LEFT at T junction by War Memorial signposted Warwick A46 East. **Cycle 0·3m to T junction end.**

48·5 LEFT onto A46. **Cycle 0·5m to first right signposted Hampton Lucey 2 ¾.**

49·0 RIGHT signposted Hampton Lucey 2 ¾. **Cycle 0·6m to crossroads end with A439.**

49·6 CONT at crossroads signposted Hampton Lucey 2 ¼. **Cycle 2·7m via Hampton Lucey to T junction end.**

52·3 RIGHT signposted Wellesbourne 1 ½. **Cycle 0·2m to 1st**

left turn signposted Wellesbourne 1 ½.

52·5 LEFT   signposted Wellesbourne 1 ½. **Cycle 0·9m to roundabout end with A42.**

53·4 CONT   over roundabout signposted Wellesbourne B4086. **Cycle 5m to T junction end in Kineton.**

58·4 RIGHT   at T junction in Kineton. **Cycle 3·2m to left turn signposted Arlescotte ½ & Avon Dasset 2.**

61·6 LEFT   signposted Arlescotte ½ & Avon Dasset 2. **Cycle 1·6m to crossroads end with B4100.**

63·2 CONT   over crossroads signposted Avon Dasset ½ & Farnborough 2 ¼. **Cycle 2·5m through Avon Dasset to T junction in Fenny Compton.**

65·7 RIGHT   at T junction signposted Wormleighton 2. **Cycle 0·1m to T junction end.**

65·8 LEFT   signposted Wormleighton 2. **Cycle 1·1m to staggered crossroads end with A423.**

66·9 CONT   (right then left) over staggered crossroads signposted Wormleighton 1 & Priors Hardwick 3. **Cycle 2m through Wormleighton to left turn signposted Priors Hardwick 1 ½.**

68·9 LEFT   signposted Priors Hardwick 1 ½. **Cycle 3·1m via Priors Hardwick to T junction in Priors Marston.**

72·0 LEFT   at T junction signposted Lower Shuckbrurgh 3. **Cycle 0·1m to 2nd right by memorial.**

72·1 RIGHT   by memorial signposted Lower Shuckbrugh 3. **Cycle 2·3m to right turn signposted Lower Shuckburgh.**

74·4 RIGHT   signposted Lower Shuckburgh 1 ¼. **Cycle 1·2m to staggered crossroads end with A425. Caution - gated road - 5 gates in all.**

75·6 CONT (right then left) over staggered crossroads signposted Willoughby 3. **Cycle 1·4m to left turn signposted Willoughby 2 ½ by a bridge over disused railway.**

77·0 LEFT signposted Willoughby 2 ½ & over rail bridge. **Cycle to 1st left turn signposted Leamington Hastings 3.**

77·1 LEFT signposted Leamington Hastings 3 ¼ (gated road). **Cycle 3m to T junction end with A426.**

80·1 LEFT at T junction signposted A426 Banbury. **Cycle 0·2m to 1st right signposted Leamington Hastings ¾.**

80·3 RIGHT signposted Leamington Hastings ¾ & Birdingbury. **Cycle 3·3m through Leamington Hastings and Birdinbury villages to T junction end with A423.**

83·6 RIGHT at T junction inMarton signposted A423 Coventry. **Cycle to 1st left turn signposted Eathorpe 1 ¼.**

84·3 LEFT signposted Eathorpe 1 ¼. **Cycle 0·4m to T junction end with B4455 Fosse Way.**

84·7 RIGHT at T junction signposted B4455 Fosse Way & Princethorpe ½. **Cycle 0·4m to crossroads.**

85·1 CONT over staggered crossroads signposted Leicester & B4455 Fosse Way. **Cycle 0·1m to 1st left turn.**

85·2 LEFT signposted Leicester & Fosse Way Stretton. **Cycle 1·8m to roundabout with A45.**

87·0 CONT over roundabout signposted Leicester & Fosse Way. **Cycle 0·9m to left turn into Dyers Lane.**

87·9 LEFT signposted Dyers Lane. **Cycle 0·7m to crossroads end in Wolston.
Caution - narrow road.**

88·6 CONT over crossroads in Wolston into road signpostedMain Street. **Cycle 0·4m to Wolston hall.**

90·0 CONT into Wolston Village Hall.

End of 90m route.

THE SUSTRANS PATH & THE YORKSHIRE WOLDS

The Yorkshire routes start and finish at York Racecourse, easily accessible from York Railway Station. The ride starts on the splendid York-Selby Sustrans cycle path which takes you from the city into open country without using a main road. The path is dotted with interesting landmarks and is 6m long.

After 20m the routes divide and the long route heads to The Wolds where after a few enjoyable climbs the reward of a great tea stop in Thixendale awaits. Alternatively, excellent food is served at The Wolds Inn at Huggate, after 37 miles. The route flattens out as you rejoin the short route after 58 miles. From here, both routes pass through the delightful village of Osbaldwick 2.5m to the east of York. The route follows more Sustrans paths before finishing with a pleasant cycle alongside the River Ouse.

Map	OS LR 100 Malton & Pickering. OS LR 105 York. OS LR 106 Market Weighton.
Distance	35 or 67 miles.
Start/Finish	The Silver Ring, York Racecourse at Knavesmire. 1.25m south of York centre.

Railway Access

York - on the north/south inter-city line and local services.

Places to see

York. A host of attractions to see in York - make the tourist information office at the railway station or Exhibition Square your first stop.

Jorvik Viking Centre, York. Built on the site of the excavation of the Viking Street of Coppergate. Visitors are whisked back 100 years to a recreation of the street. Hugely popular.

York Minster. The largest medieval Gothic cathedral in Northern Europe.

National Railway Museum. Experience the history of the railways and the way they shaped the world. Not just for train-spotters.

Osbaldwick. A pretty village east of York.

Yorkshire Wolds. Natural splendour east of York.

Huggate & Thixendale. Villages in the wolds, on the long route.

Tourist Information Office, railway station concourse 0904 643700. Exhibition Square, York 0904 621756.

Refreshments

Wenlock Arms PH, Weldrake - 12.4m, short route.

Derwent Arms PH, Osbaldwick - 30m, 61.6m.

Wolds Inn, Huggate - 37m.

Pub and Tea shops, Thixendale - 41.6m.

Tea shops galore and the famous Betty's, York.

YORKSHIRE   THE SUSTRANS PATH &
THE YORKSHIRE WOLDS

York

Derwent Arms PH

Holtby

58·1m

A166

Dunnington

Osbaldwick

A1079

B1228

Start & Finish

A64

20·2m
Routes Divide

35m

67m

B1222

A19

1·6m

Wenlock Arms PH

Weldrake

12·4m

York - Selby Cycle Path

N

Escrick

R. Ouse

Thorganby

Skipwith

Rickall

8·9m

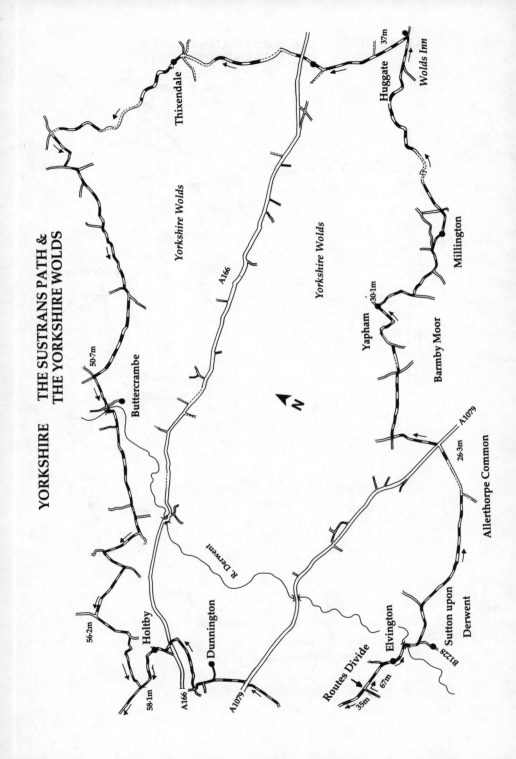

YORKSHIRE - 35M ROUTE

0·0   RIGHT   out of York race course. **Cycle 0·1m to the start
of the Sustrans York to Selby cycle path by the
white sign and red bars ahead and on your right.**

0·1   RIGHT   onto cycle path by white signpost reading Leeds A64.
Cycle 0·5m to the red bars on the path.

0·6   RIGHT   at red bars by signpost for signposted Selby via
Railway Path. **Cross the racecourse and follow the
path for 0·7m to a left turn which goes under a
bridge over the A64 on your left.**

1·3   LEFT   onto path which passes under the bridge ahead on
your left, the path runs parallel to the A64.
Cycle 0·3m to more red bars.

1·6   LEFT   at red bars under another bridge. **Cycle along the
path for 0·4m to its end at a housing estate.**

2·0   CONT   at the end of the path into the road ahead Appleton
Court. **Cycle 0·2m to rejoin the path.**

2·2   CONT   through red gates and rejoin the path. **Cycle 5·9m
along the Sustrans path to red bars near the
A19 at Riccall.**

8·1   CONT   through red bars alongside A19. **Cycle 0·2m to
T junction end on the edge of Riccall.**

8·3   RIGHT   at T junction and enter Riccall.
Cycle 0·3m to traffic lights in Riccall.

8·6   LEFT   at these traffic lights into Station Road.
Cycle 0·3m to the wooden fence ahead.

8·9   CONT   at wooden fence by **dismounting** your bike and **walk
when clear** over the busy A19 and into the minor
road ahead. This road is King Rudding Lane. **Cycle
3m to T junction end with a B road. This road has
1m of hard but bumpy surface when it becomes
narrow.**

11·9 CONT as the small road joins a B road in Skipwith. Follow the road with the pond on your left and the PH on your right. **Cycle 0·5m to right turn signposted Thorganby 3, Wheldrake 5 & Elvington 8.**

12·4 RIGHT signposted Thorganby 3, Wheldrake 5 & Elvington 8. **Cycle 5·4ms to a right turn in Wheldrake by the PH.**

17·8 RIGHT in Wheldrake signposted Elvington 3. **Cycle 2·4m to T junction end.**

20·2 LEFT at T junction signposted Dunnington 4. **Cycle 1·5m to a right turn signposted Dunnington 2. (You may prefer to cycle on the pavement until the road widens later).**

The longer route turns right here.

21·7 RIGHT signposted Dunnington 2 & Hull. **Cycle 1·7m to T junction end.**

23·0 CONT over staggered crossroads with busy A1079 to the small road ahead signposted Dunnington, 1 into Common Road. **Cycle 0·9m to crossroads in Dunnington village.**

23·9 CONT over crossroads in Dunnington by Cross Keys PH. **Cycle 0·2m to right turn into Eastfield Lane.**

24·1 RIGHT into Eastfield Lane. **Cycle 0·8m to T junction end.**

25·3 LEFT at T junction with busy A166. **Walk your bike along the grass to the bus shelter ahead to immediate right turn signposted 'Unsuitable for Heavy Vehicles.'**

25·3 RIGHT into small road opposite the bus shelter onto road signposted 'Unsuitable for Heavy Vehicles.' **Cycle 0·1m to T junction at the bottom of this road.**

25·5 RIGHT at T junction and into Holtby. **Cycle 0·2m to left turn signposted Stockton On Forest 3.**

25·7   LEFT   signposted Stockton On Forest 3. **Cycle 1·5m to a
left turn signposted Murton 1 ½.**

27·2   LEFT   signpostedMurton 1 ½. **Cycle 1·5m to a right
turn in Murton just past a red telephone box.**

28·7   RIGHT   in Murton just past the telephone box. **Cycle 1·3m to
right turn in Osbaldwick just after the Derwent
Arms PH.**

30·0   RIGHT   just after Derwent Arms PH onto small road
signposted Metcalfe Lane, Private Road. **Cycle 0·1m
to entrance to Sustrans cycle path with red gates.**

30·1   LEFT   and onto the cycle path. **Cycle 1·1m along the
path to just before its end. Here we pick up 200
metres of unsurfaced path heading towards the
Parcel Force building, which you will be able to see
on your right.**

31·2   CONT   onto unsurfaced path heading towards the Parcel
Force building ahead of you. **Walk or cycle with this
building to your immediate right until you shortly
rejoin the paved cycle path.**

31·3   CONT   back onto the paved Sustrans cycle path.
**Cycle 1·2m to the end of this path as it exits near a
junction with traffic lights.**

31·5   LEFT   at this junction and onto Crichton Avenue and over a
bridge. **Cycle 0·1m to the first left urn.**

31·6   LEFT   into unsignposted road. **Cycle 0·6m to T junction
end.**

32·2   LEFT   at T junction. **Cycle 0·3m to the third right turn, St
Mary's cul-de-sac. This turn is by the second
pedestrian crossing.**

32·5   RIGHT   into St Mary's cul-de-sac by using the pedestrian
crossing. **Cycle 0·1m to some steps leading to a
bike path by a grey fence at the bottom of this road.**

32·6   CONT   by walking down the 6 steps. **Follow the bike path along the grey fence ahead and on your right to a bridge over the river in 0·1m.**

32·7   CONT   by walking over the bridge, use the concrete bike ramps to go over the bridge.

32·8   LEFT   on the other bank of the river onto your third Sustrans bike path. **Cycle 0·3m along the path until it finishes at a crossroads on North Street with traffic lights.**

33·1   CONT   over traffic lights into Skeldergate towards Sustrans Restaurant ahead. **Cycle 0·2m to a left turn onto a marked cycle path which goes under a bridge.**

33·3   LEFT   and onto cycle way which passes under a bridge. **Cycle 1·0m along the tarmac by the river path until it turns away leading to some small white bars.**

34·3   CONT   through these white bars and up the small rise to the front of the Terrys Chocolate factory.

34·4   LEFT   along the bike path for 100 metres following the road to the crossing signposted Selby.

34·4   CROSS ROAD and cycle through the red bars ahead. **Cycle 0·2m along the path to the road which takes you back to the Knavesmire & the Silver Ring.**

End of 35 mile route.

YORKSHIRE - 67M ROUTE

0·0   RIGHT out of York race course. **Cycle 0·1m to the start of the Sustrans York to Selby cycle path by the white sign and red bars ahead and on your right.**

0·1   RIGHT onto cycle path by white signpost reading Leeds A64. **Cycle 0·5m to the red bars on the path.**

0·6   RIGHT at red bars by signpost for signposted Selby via Railway Path. **Cross racecourse and follow the path for 0·7m to a left turn which goes under a bridge over the A64 on your left.**

1·3   LEFT onto path which passes under the bridge ahead on your left, the path runs parallel to the A64. **Cycle 0·3m to more red bars.**

1·6   LEFT at red bars under another bridge. **Cycle along the path for 0·4m to its end at a housing estate.**

2·0   CONT at the end of the path into the road ahead - Appleton Court. **Cycle 0·2m to rejoin the path.**

2·2   CONT through red gates and rejoin the path. **Cycle 5·9m along the Sustrans path to some red bars near the A19 at Riccall.**

8·1   CONT through red bars alongside A19. **Cycle 0·2m to T junction on the edge of Riccall.**

8·3   RIGHT at T junction and enter Riccall. **Cycle 0·3m to traffic lights in Riccall.**

8·6   LEFT at these traffic lights into Station Road. **Cycle 0·3m to the wooden fence ahead.**

8·9   CONT at wooden fence by **dismounting** your bike and **walking when clear** over the busy A19 and into the minor road ahead. This road is King Rudding Lane. **Cycle 3m to T junction end with a B road. This road has 1m of hard but bumpy surface when it becomes narrow.**

11·9 CONT as the small road joins a B road in Skipwith. Follow the road with the pond on your left and the PH on your right. **Cycle 0·5m to 2nd right turn signposted Thorganby 3, Wheldrake 5 & Elvington 8.**

12·4 RIGHT signposted Thorganby 3, Wheldrake 5 & Elvington 8. **Cycle 5·4m to a right turn in Wheldrake.**

17·8 RIGHT in Wheldrake signposted Elvington 3. **Cycle 2·4m to T junction end.**

20·2 RIGHT at T junction signposted Elvington ½. **Cycle 1·4m to left turn signposted Newton Upon Derwent.**

20·2 *The short route turns left here.*

22·2 LEFT signposted Newton Upon Derwent, Wilberfoss & Pocklington. **Cycle 4·1m to crossroads end.**

26·3 CONT over crossroads with A1079 onto road signposted Stamford Bridge 6. **Cycle 0·9m to first right turn signposted Yapham.**

27·2 RIGHT signposted Yapham 2. **Cycle 1·3m to T junction.**

28·5 CONT over staggered crossroads onto road signposted Bishop Wilton 4 & Yapham 1. **Cycle 0·5m to T junction end**

29·0 LEFT at T junction signposted Yapham,Meltonby. **Cycle 1·1m to right turn signposted Pocklington 2 ½.**

30·1 RIGHT signposted Pocklington 2 ½. **Cycle 0·8m to first unsignposted left turn.**

30·9 LEFT into unsignposted lane. **Cycle 0·6m to T junction.**

31·6 LEFT at T junction beside houses on a bend. **Cycle 0·3m to first right turn signposted Millington 1.**

31·9 RIGHT signpostedMillington 1, Huggate 5. **Cycle 4·4m to T junction end by a Give Way sign.**

36·3 LEFT at T junction with Give Way sign. **Cycle 0·7m**

to first left turn signposted York.

37·0 LEFT signposted York & Fridaythorpe, just before Huggate. **Cycle 1·8m to first right signposted Thixendale.**

38·8 RIGHT by large stones signposted Thixendale 3. **Cycle 0·4m to crossroads with A166.**

39·2 CONT over A166 onto road signposted Thixendale. **Cycle 2·4m to the T junction end. Caution - steep descent ahead.**

41·6 RIGHT at T junction signposted Thixendale (to your right). **Cycle to immediate left turn signposted Birdsall 5.**

41·6 LEFT signposted Birdsall 5. **Cycle 3·5m through Thixendale and up the valley to a crossroads signposted Acklam 2.**

45·2 LEFT at crossroads signposted Acklam 2, Pocklington 12. **Cycle 0·8m to T junction end.**

46·0 LEFT at T junction signposted Pocklington 11. **Cycle 0·2m to first right signposted Acklam 1 & Barthorpe.**

46·2 RIGHT signposted Acklam 1 & Barthorpe 2 ½. **Cycle 2·5m to a right turn signposted York 12 & Scrayingham 3. Caution - very steep descents ahead.**

48·9 RIGHT signposted York 12, Scrayingham 3. **Cycle 1·8m to a crossroads end.**

50·7 LEFT at crossroads signposted Stamford Bridge 3 & Pocklington 8. **Cycle 3·2m to the fourth turn on your right which has a broken signpost and a farm on the corner with a large green silo visible.**

53·9 RIGHT into turn with broken sign and by farm with green silo. **Cycle 0·8m to T junction end.**

54·7 LEFT at T junction signposted Gate Helmsley 1 ¼ & York 7 ¾ . **Cycle 0·5m to first right signposted Warthill.**

55·2 RIGHT signposted Warthill 1 ½. **Cycle 1·0m to T junction.**

56·2 LEFT at T junction signposted Gate Helmsley 1 ¾ & Stamford Bridge 3. **Cycle 0·8m to first right signposted Local Traffic Only.**

57·0 RIGHT signposted Local Traffic Only. **Cycle 0·3m to T junction end.**

58·1 RIGHT at T junction signposted York 4 ½. **Cycle 0·7m to first left signposted Murton 1 ½.**

The 35 mile route rejoins here.

58·8 LEFT signposted Murton 1 ½. **Cycle 1·5m to a right turn in Murton just past a red telephone box.**

60·3 RIGHT in Murton just past the red telephone box. **Cycle 1·3m to right turn in Osbaldwick just after the Derwent Arms PH.**

61·6 RIGHT just after Derwent Arms PH onto small road signposted Metcalfe Lane, Private Road. **Cycle 0·1m to entrance to Sustrans cycle path with red gates.**

61·7 LEFT and onto the cycle path. **Cycle 1·1m along the path to just before its end. Here we pick up 200 metres of unsurfaced path heading towards the Parcel Force building which you can see.**

62·8 CONT onto unsurfaced path heading towards the Parcel Force building ahead of you. **Walk or cycle with this building to your immediate right until you shortly rejoin the paved cycle path.**

62·9 CONT back onto the paved Sustrans cycle path. **Cycle 1·2m to the end of this path as it exits near a junction with traffic lights.**

64·1 LEFT at this junction and onto Crichton Avenue and over a bridge. **Cycle 0·1m to the first left turn.**

64·5 LEFT into unsignposted road. **Cycle 0·6m to T junction.**

65·1 LEFT at T junction. **Cycle 0·3m to the third right turn into St Mary's cul-de-sac.** This turn is by the second pedestrian crossing.

65·4 RIGHT into St Mary's cul-de-sac by using the pedestrian crossing. **Cycle 0·1m to some steps leading to a bike path by a grey fence at the bottom of this road.**

65·5 CONT by walking down the 6 steps. **Follow the bike path for 0·1m along the grey fence ahead and on your right to a bridge over the river.**

65·6 CONT by walking over the bridge, use the concrete bike ramps.

65·7 LEFT on the other bank of the river onto your third Sustrans bike path. **Cycle 0·3m along the path until its end at a crossroads with traffic lights on North Street.**

66·0 CONT over traffic lights into Skeldergate towards Sustrans Restaurant ahead. **Cycle 0·2m to a left turn onto a marked cycle path which goes under a bridge.**

66·2 LEFT and onto cycle way which passes under a bridge. **Cycle 1·0m along the river following the tarmac path until it turns away from the river and leads to some small white bars.**

67·2 CONT through these white bars and up the small rise to the front of the Terrys Chocolate factory.

67·2 LEFT along the bike path for 100 metres following the road to the crossing signposted Selby.

67·4 CONT at crossing and cycle through the red bars ahead. **Cycle 0·2m along the path to the road which takes you back to the Silver Ring.**

67·6 back at the Silver Ring at the Knavesmire.

End of 67m route.

TWO WHEELS

BREATHING SPACES - Bike Rides Within Easy Reach of London - Patrick Field.

24 bike rides, easily reached from London by car or by train. A great mix of on and off-road routes, all day rides for mountain bikers and tourers, leisurely country lanes and family rides. With route maps, details of places to see and refreshment stops. *Pbk, 170pp, £7.99.*

Cox's Rural Rides - 36 tours in the south-east - Tim Cox.

The choice of tours ranges from short excursions to challenging day trips - routes can easily be linked to form longer routes. The illustrated descriptions include details of places to see, fascinating local history and where to stop for food and drink. *Pbk, 272pp, £8.99.*

Haute-Savoie & Mont Blanc - Mountain Bike Guide - Cassani & Lamory.

Discover one of the best kept mountain biking secrets in Europe - from the southern shore of Lake Geneva to the Mont Blanc area. A selection of 50 routes from challenging high level rides, to superb forest tracks and gentle low level excursions. *Pbk, 192pp, £8.99.*

GET LOST - Off-Road Adventures With A Bicycle Within Easy Reach Of London - Patrick Field.

An off-road follow up to Breathing Spaces, packed with great escapes from London and the suburbs to the countryside. *Pbk, 192pp, £7.99.*

Available from all good bookshops or direct from the publisher plus £1 postage & packing per copy. Two Heads Publishing, 12A Franklyn Suite, The Priory, Haywards Heath, West Sussex, RH16 3LB.

TWO WHEELS

BREATHING SPACES - Bike Rides Within Easy Reach of London - Patrick Field.

24 bike rides, easily reached from London by car or by train. A great mix of on and off-road routes, all day rides for mountain bikers and tourers, leisurely country lanes and family rides. With route maps, details of places to see and refreshment stops. *Pbk, 170pp, £7.99.*

Cox's Rural Rides - 36 tours in the south-east - Tim Cox.

The choice of tours ranges from short excursions to challenging day trips - routes can easily be linked to form longer routes. The illustrated descriptions include details of places to see, fascinating local history and where to stop for food and drink. *Pbk, 272pp, £8.99.*

Haute-Savoie & Mont Blanc - Mountain Bike Guide - Cassani & Lamory.

Discover one of the best kept mountain biking secrets in Europe - from the southern shore of Lake Geneva to the Mont Blanc area. A selection of 50 routes from challenging high level rides, to superb forest tracks and gentle low level excursions. *Pbk, 192pp, £8.99.*

GET LOST - Off-Road Adventures With A Bicycle Within Easy Reach Of London - Patrick Field.

An off-road follow up to Breathing Spaces, packed with great escapes from London and the suburbs to the countryside. *Pbk, 192pp, £7.99.*

Available from all good bookshops or direct from the publisher plus £1 postage & packing per copy. Two Heads Publishing, 12A Franklyn Suite, The Priory, Haywards Heath, West Sussex, RH16 3LB.